INTROVERT TO AMBIVERT

BUILDING PEOPLE SKILLS FOR SUCCESS IN BUSINESS AND IN LIFE

By Edwin Palsma & Vy Tri Truong

Copyright © 2017 by Edwin Palsma & Vy Tri Truong

All rights reserved. This book or any portion thereof may not be reproduced or used in any manner whatsoever without the express written permission of the publisher. The publication contains the opinions and ideas of its authors and is intended for informational purposes only.

First Printing, 2015

www.facebook.com/ambivertjourney

Table of Contents

Foreword

Introduction	1
Edwin's Story	7
Vy Tri's Story	25
The Ambivert Advantage	39
Weirdoverts	51
Beginning Your Journey	65
Small Talk	83
Talking to Strangers	109
Selling for Ambiverts	127
Putting it All Together	149
Join Us	157

Foreword

It figures that two introverts who co-authored a book would need to explain the book before you start reading it.

If you picked up this book, you most likely already understand the term "ambivert." We like to define it as someone who is both an introvert and an extrovert. They have a good mix of both personality types, and can adapt as the situation requires.

In this book, we share our stories about how we two introverts became ambiverts. It explores our lessons gleaned and pitfalls to avoid.

Also, both of us being Canadian, we thought we should use this space to apologize in advance in case you find anything in the book offensive.

In all seriousness though, this book is a bit different in that we two writers have dissimilar writing styles. Rather than try to mesh the two so that it gives one consistent voice throughout the book, we decided that it is better to leave our personal writing styles intact. The reasoning (or fault) in our logic is that, when it comes to personal development, people need to hear things in multiple ways until one of those ways "clicks" with them and they "get it." It is our hope that, because we combine words in our own unique ways, you will find that one of those combinations actually makes sense to you.

And because we are looking to grow more ourselves, we would love to hear about your introvert to ambivert journeys as well. The way you combine words and your unique background could be the key that helps us or another person find success in their journey. Please do reach out. More on this at the end of the book in the *Join Us* section.

Introduction

By Vy Tri

Extroverts just have more fun. There, I said it.

I think somewhere in the middle of high school that thought resonated in my brain. Of course, at the time I had no idea about the terms introvert and extrovert, let alone ambivert. I just knew that some kids had the right personality and the right attitude. I wanted those traits for myself.

So I made a decision: I would "come out of my shell" and become more sociable. And thus began my long (long) journey where I slowly changed, evolved, and ultimately became a "people person." It wasn't until other people started calling me "outgoing" that I realized that I had actually moved past just being an introvert.

Without any clear direction, guide, or plan of attack, it took a long time and a lot of trial and error. I spent a lot of time as a "weirdovert." I cover this in a lot more detail later, but here's a quick definition: You know the people in your life who are just a little too loud and excited? The annoying not so fun extrovert? Yup, that's a weirdovert.

So to help you avoid time in weirdovert land, Edwin and I decided to write this book. We both went through the process without a roadmap, and it was painful.

When I first met Edwin, I thought he was an extrovert. He displayed all the characteristics, except that he was always a little more intellectual and in-depth about everything. Edwin did not seem shy. He loved to network, gave presentations, and taught classes. For the better part of a decade, I pegged him as an extrovert.

One day I attended a presentation by Doug Bolger (iLearn2.com) and discovered the missing link in my thought routines. Doug showed us how we were born with different personalities and how it was okay. He described how one type is different than another, but not necessarily better. Doug was so funny that I spent the entire 2-hr presentation trying to hold my gut in.

So I came back to Edwin, pegging him as an "orange" personality, which was supposed to be the most extroverted personality type. To my surprise, Edwin said he was actually a green and quite introverted. What the heck? I didn't know what to make of it.

Over the next few days and weeks, the thoughts just kept rolling in my head. If both Edwin and I are introverts whom people think are extroverts, then how many of us are there? And how many of us are on the same journey? How many of us have been lost without a road map?

So we decided to write this book. Part of it was to see just how many people like us there were in the world. Part of it was to help those people and establish a support network. But the real reason (and you know you've really become an extrovert when this is your motivation) is to get on The Ellen DeGenres Show. Or to get on TV with Oprah. We're not sure which we one we prefer. Ellen will make us dance (very scary for introverts) and Oprah will make us cry (also very scary for introverts).

If, after reading this book, you've found that it helped you (and you work for Oprah or Ellen) we would ask that you help us get to our goals as well. Heck, we would even kiss your feet if you got us on Breakfast Television. But we digress.

So who is this book for?

This book is for those of you who were born introverts but you want to be more outgoing, more of a people person. Your friends tell you that you need to come out of your shell and just loosen up. If anyone has ever told you "Dude, there's chicks all around and you want to go home and play HALO?" then this book is for you. (True story, this happened to me. Thanks, BP.)

If you want to stay true to yourself and embrace your serious, quiet, and reflective nature, this is NOT the book for you. There is nothing wrong with being an introvert and staying an introvert. And if that's what you want, God bless you, all the more power to you. That is totally cool, and we mean it. But that's not what you'll find in these pages. There are other books you can find to empower you to be a better you. For instance, read Susan Cain's book *Quiet: The Power of Introverts In A World That Can't Stop Talking*. It's great; you'll love it.

Read our book because you want to change, not because you want to be more comfortable in your own skin and really "find yourself." This book is not about living within yourself or being happy with who you are. It's for those of you who are not satisfied with the personality you were born with. Read this if want to live life on the other side.

This book is about change. And we don't mean the "order the salad instead of the burger" kind of change. We mean the gut-wrenching, transforming, "cry yourself to sleep" kind of change. We promise you that you will cry when you embark on this journey. Both tears of joy and tears of embarrassment.

True change requires desire; you have to want the lifestyle, money, power, influence, or sex-appeal that goes with extroversion. Whatever your goal or reason behind wanting to change, it has to be real to you. It has to gnaw at you and cause you to do the uncomfortable and the unnatural. It has to be a huge vision or goal.

Nothing in these pages is easy. The theories are simple and the ask will be simple, but the execution will not be easy. You will put yourself through many, many uncomfortable and awkward moments during your journey. On many occasions you will find yourself curled up in the fetal position wondering if it will ever happen for you. It will be a multi-year endeavour to complete the transformation.

But you know what? It can be done. So many people who you think are extroverts are actually introverts in disguise. And that's all you need to know. If it's been done by others, it can be done by you.

Our way isn't the only way, but it's worked for us. Use the "shopping cart" method. Take what you like, leave everything else on the shelf. Re-read this book every couple of years and see if your grocery selection has changed.

You will also come across other ideas as you go on your journey. Don't be afraid of implementing those suggestions too. Remember, at your core, you are an introvert, so run any idea through your analytical mind. See if it fits you.

The most important thing is that you start doing something. Start your journey. Keep trying things, keep growing, keep sharing.

Edwin and I felt it was important to start this book with our own personal journeys because it is through stories that knowledge and lessons can truly be conveyed. Our stories were not easy to write as many aspects of them were quite embarrassing. However, we hope that you can relate a bit and possibly find some encouragement in our failures as you embark on your journey.

We hope that through these pages, you will find the power and confidence necessary to make the changes in your life in order to achieve your dreams and goals. Edwin and I write this book in good faith. We have no idea if it will sell or not. That is not the goal.

The goal is to impart knowledge and help people. If we do our jobs, and help enough people then we will get our rewards. And if we've helped you, please, pay it forward.

Congratulations on your decision and welcome to the first day of the rest of your life.

Edwin's Story

When Vy Tri asked me to help him with this book, I decided to first ask my friends if they thought I was an extrovert or introvert. Other than really close friends, everyone thinks I'm an extrovert. Success! I've managed to bury exactly who I am!

Actually, not at all. I am exactly who I want to be – an introvert by nature and an extrovert when needed. I have learned that there is a time and a place for each part of me to come out, and I'm continually getting better at using them in the right situations. I actually enjoy being both, and I have found that I *need* to be both – neither one is useful all the time.

My close friends see my default self when I'm resting and relaxing. They see me more often and for longer periods of time. They see me let my guard down. I get to unwind and know that they will accept my quietness. They know my need to just get away from the bustle and exist in a simpler, less chaotic place.

An ambivert is an introvert by nature and an extrovert when needed.

At parties, I don't have to fake it anymore. Because I am now more comfortable in my own skin, I don't hide my real personality. While I spend some time dancing because that is fun, I often seek out others who are bored with the noise and chaos and just want to sit and chat or go play ping-pong. There are many people looking for an out, and I'm happy to pass the time visiting with them. And the best part is that my friends know who I am and accept it.

But in my outside world, where I meet lots of people, most think I'm an extrovert. They're surprised when I tell them the truth. How I've evolved wasn't easy, took a long time, and is still ongoing.

Each of us is born with characteristics of introversion and extroversion and one aspect usually dominates. When I look back, my qualities of introversion were really apparent.

Finding the right balance is complicated.

Growing up on a farm, the repetitive and focused work immersed me in a life that my soul just loved. Driving the tractor for hours with my talk radio for a companion was fun. The concentration required to plow perfectly straight rows or pack the silage just right was an invigorating challenge. Feeding the cows and calves, hauling manure or mowing the lawn were times of solitude that I looked forward to. Even now, twenty years after moving away, I still enjoy getting on the tractor or dump truck and just going to work. I even enjoy losing myself in the quiet and dark of a welding helmet and fixing things.

Play time on the farm was also focused. Usually it was just my brother and me. We would ride our bikes, climb fences, or go back into the pasture and play tag on our motorcycles. Shooting gophers or trapping moles was also fun. I liked being around him. Even playing with my sisters was fun. I loved the simplicity of hanging out with just one or two other people.

Air Cadets was the one other place that I felt most comfortable. My goal was to be a pilot like my Dad and get my license for free. I didn't know at the time, but it was a place of refuge for me. I spent many of my evenings in the quietness of marching, classes, and paperwork. There isn't a lot of stimuli at any one time. It's very focused, linear work, with not a lot of distraction. I was successful, here, because my work aligned with my natural bent.

My second life was the chaotic one that is school and sports. Here, I could tell that you needed to be outgoing to be liked and successful.

At the time, I didn't have the self-awareness to see what I looked like from the outside. One of my best friends growing up was Rob. We reconnected recently after not seeing each other for twelve years. Rob told me that he remembered me being very confident. He said it was a bit attractive, but at the same time, a little off putting.

When I look back, I can see that I was putting on a front. School seemed easy, and I was reasonably athletic (easier in a small school). I became cocky as my way of trying to be bold and fit in. As a ten year old, that seemed like a good idea and there wasn't anyone telling or coaching me any different. Right through middle school and into high school, it was the only way that I knew how to fit in.

When I see those types of kids today, I feel very empathetic. I know that most of them have developed it as a pattern of life to compensate for feeling uncomfortable when around other people. I was the person who put on a brave front, attacking conversations and groups of people, rather than simply rolling with life. I didn't want to get called out as boring or quiet.

My journey to breaking that habit of cockiness started one afternoon on the bus ride home from high school. The conversation that I had was so impactful that I even remember where the bus was; just coming up the hill out of Ponoka on Highway 53. One of my best friends, Eric, turned to me and told me that I was an ass. He said I was a cocky S.O.B. and that people were starting to dislike me.

Of course, my immediate reaction was to be pissed off. However, one of the characteristics of introverts is that we are thoughtful (meaning we spend too much time in our own heads) and so I didn't just brush off the comment. Even then, I could see the truth of such a statement but had no idea what to do with it. I think that I toned things down a bit for the rest of my high school years, but it took many more years and many more comments from other influential people for me to become who I am today. It was also a turning point for me in that I recognized that the people around me are able to speak truths into my life so I'm always listening for these gems of wisdom.

We will talk a bit later in this book about "resetting" as a popular change mechanism for introverts moving towards ambiversion. For me, that first step started when I left for university. I escaped my hometown and went to a place where I knew no one – Trinity Western University in Langley, BC. I could get a new start because I didn't have any history to overcome.

Accept yourself.

My first roommate, Pat, was a true blue introvert and was comfortable in who he was. From him I learned it wasn't necessary to hide who I was. I started to recognize and enjoy my times of escape. I liked the quietness of our dorm room as a place to read or nap.

I signed up for the 8AM classes because it was much quieter then. The cafeteria and sidewalks were empty. I enjoyed going to the library and studying in small groups. I liked spending time in the gym shooting hoops by myself.

I also had the benefit of a very healthy extrovert in my best friend Dave. I didn't have to work as hard at extroversion when Dave was around because I would just follow his lead. If you asked the majority of people at Trinity Western, they would probably characterize me as an extrovert because of the antics we got up to.

Because many of my moments of extroversion didn't work (like most university students I did some stupid things) I learned one of the most valuable lessons about human nature. People give you a lot of grace when you put yourself out there. Dave and I did a lot of wild and crazy things – singing outside of girls' dorms, being loud, wrestling in the snow, crazy haircuts, and more.

And most people are ok and even like to see that. My theory is that introverts look at those behaviours and wish they could do them, and extroverts like seeing other people who act like themselves. As long as what you are doing isn't hurting anyone, you can do a lot of things and people will accept it.

Through my university summers, back in Alberta, I reverted more to my introverted self. The first summer I worked in an office doing number crunching and accounting. The following years I did construction, building grain elevators across the Prairies. Each summer gave me a couple of months to recharge my introverted self before going back to school and being outgoing.

Through both my school and my summers, I learned to adapt to my surroundings. I learned how to be less cocky and more relaxed (though I'm far from perfect in either of these areas). I learned that there are many other people who are just like me. And I learned that there are times and places to be introverted or extroverted.

When I got engaged, I moved to a less transient job in Edmonton and settled down. By luck, I ended up working for my own financial advisor, Jack. My first task was to write a book for him, a perfect job for an introvert. I spent most days quietly cooped up in an office reading, researching, and writing.

I also went with Jack to his speaking events. He had built his own speaking career, teaching about finances in churches. In addition to learning more about what he wanted to include in his book, I also learned public speaking from a true master. And it's where I learned another amazing lesson.

Extroversion is like a muscle that you can build up over time.

For short periods of time, no matter how uncomfortable you are, you can act however you want. It will likely take a lot of energy, but it can be done. Extroversion is like a muscle that you can build up over time. If I asked you to experiment with extroversion at a party or other social function, at first you could do it for a short time. Maybe you only have the energy to do it for five minutes or maybe fifteen. But you can do it. Over time, you will be able to do it for longer as you build up your extroversion muscle.

Public speaking is a great way to work on that muscle. When up on a stage or in front of a class, many times, just being up there makes people like you. The audience automatically thinks you are outgoing and friendly. The audience believes it takes a special person to do public speaking, as it's one of the most common phobias. They think you are an extrovert.

When Jack asked me to do some teaching with him, I jumped right in. I am always eager to try things and this was a skill I didn't have yet. Because I'm also a bit of a perfectionist, I asked a few close friends to spend an evening in my office and give me feedback while I practiced teaching. I even filmed a few of my classes to see what I looked like. I was lucky in that I was able to really ease into this, starting with a five minute fully prepared speech that slowly increased over two years until I was doing three-hour presentations on my own.

In building my extrovert muscle, I learned two rules. The first was the Pareto Principle or the 80/20 rule. It states that 80% of the impact of something comes from 20% of the effort. It's a commonly used businesses idea: 80% of a company's profit comes from 20% of the clients; 80% of the Human Resource problems come from 20% of the employees.

For introverts, only 20% of your time needs to be extroverted to make an 80% impact on people's perception of you. So, for that 20% of your time, can you work hard at something that doesn't come naturally? Can you work at it if that 20% of your time likely correlates strongly with 80% of your success in business and life? Public speaking is that short intense burst of time that can set the stage for all the rest of your interactions with people.

From writing a book on finances for Jack to becoming an assistant financial advisor was a natural progression. But it's a different role as it's meeting with individuals and talking about their money. I quickly learned that giving good financial advice does not guarantee that I will be a successful advisor.

To be successful required the second rule.

The key to influencing people is to genuinely like them.

People will only listen and act on your advice if they connect with you. It's like the old adage, "people don't care how much you know until they know how much you care." And introverts don't always come across as caring.

This is a key principle when working with people. I first read about it in Dale Carnegie's book, *How to Win Friends and Influence People*. Despite the seemingly manipulative title of the book, Dale Carnegie has one point that he iterates over and over. It's that the key to influencing people is that you have to genuinely like them. There is no gaming the system here. If you are faking, they will sense it. That is when you get labeled as a sleazy salesman.

Learning to care about people is as much a skill as anything else. Some people are naturally born to it. I wasn't. I spent all my time in my own head, rarely thinking about others. But over time, I have gotten better at it. I've learned that at the end of the day, relationships are the key to happiness and a fulfilled life. It's a strange thing to say, but the more I've worked at liking people, the more I like people.

Many people, introverts and extroverts, miss this critical part to success. We will talk about "fake it till you become it" a little later in this book, and the idea of caring works even in this area. But the "become it" part is key. You can't fake it forever. People eventually see through you.

In 2003, I moved back to BC. I was able to secure office space in Abbotsford, where I started my own financial advisory practice.

When it is the difference between starving and putting food on the table, you are forced to learn and do what works. And being extroverted worked. It was hard work, but the more I did it, the easier it got.

I didn't have a huge network of contacts when I moved here so I did the only thing I knew, which was to teach courses at the local college. In three to nine hours, I had to convince strangers that I knew what I was talking about with respect to finances, and I also had to get them to like me.

Nervousness is normal.

It was at that time that I joined Toastmasters to help refine my speaking. But Toastmasters is not just about giving speeches. Toastmasters International is a non-profit educational organization that operates clubs worldwide for the purpose of helping members improve their communication, public speaking, and leadership skills.

It is a great organization for learning how to be an extrovert. It is about learning to talk to other people, both when you are doing small talk before and after the event, but also in groups. They also teach you how to listen because soon you will be grading others on their talks.

To my surprise, the more I did public speaking, the more I enjoyed it. I'm still a bit nervous before every talk, but all that tells me is that it's something that is important. If I didn't get nervous, I wouldn't be taking it seriously. And the best part is that public speaking is the easiest way to get people to think you are outgoing – a great first impression.

Another step in my move to ambiversion was something I didn't plan but just happened. I was a volunteer with Big Brothers Big Sisters (BBBS) as a way to give back to my community and a way to practice parenting before I had kids of my own (funny but true). During my 2nd year volunteering, I was asked to join the board of the local BBBS agency.

Here I was forced to come out of my shell even more as we discussed the mentoring movement and how we were going to impact children's lives. I was fortunate that the people on this board were very engaging so they really helped me to get out of my shell. I was able to work more on the skills of extroversion in small groups which moved me even more to ambiversion.

A board is a great environment for an introvert looking to practice their extroversion. I think that introverts have an advantage on a board because they are usually intent listeners. I'm not saying that we like to just sit and listen all day. When it comes to something that we care about, we are good at focusing, listening and processing what we are hearing. We don't feel the need to pipe up and share our opinions right away. We are happy to sit and mull over an idea.

In a group setting, like a board, an introvert's challenge will be to share their ideas in a way that they get heard. Usually we have an idea but are scared to share it – which makes people think we don't have an opinion.

In two studies, Anderson and Kilduff (2009) from the University of California, Berkeley, looked at how individuals became leaders of a group. They found that the person who talks earliest and the most is perceived to be the most competent and is likely to become the leader. It has nothing to do with the quality of their suggestions. This makes it an uphill challenge for an introvert as our inclination is to not speak up unless we are confident in our opinion (and sometimes not even then). Part of the journey toward ambiversion is recognizing when our own introverted tendencies are hurting us. Sometimes we have to learn to speak up, even we aren't ready or confident.

After a few years on the local BBBS board, I was asked to attend the National Convention to represent the local board and it was a bit scary (actually it was a lot scary). Over 300 people that I didn't know walking around in a small convention center, sharing meals, sitting together in sessions, and spending time in the bar in the evenings. Not my idea of a great time (though I do love to learn so the sessions were great).

Once again, being in a brand new environment, I decided to not be myself, and I was pleasantly surprised. I actually enjoyed it. It was fun to talk to people, play some darts, learn about their lives and make new friends.

And I learned three strategies that I still use today. First, I make sure that I have some alone time. At these annual conventions, our rooms were in the same building as the sessions so I was able to go back there for some 'me' time, just to watch TV, nap, or read. I also went to the gym and pool to get an hour of uninterrupted silence.

Second, I tried to engage other people into talking about themselves and viewed each interaction as an opportunity to learn something new. Whether it was about another part of the country, another job or another role in an agency, there are lots of things I could learn. I'm insanely curious so I love to hear about the life experiences of other people. Everyone has something important to teach me.

The third thing is that having something worth remarking on makes it easier to start conversations. I learned this by accident as I was getting dressed after a nap. For whatever reason, I found a golf tee in my pocket, and I absentmindedly put it behind my ear. As I entered the next session, someone came up and commented on the tee and a conversation started about golf. Rather than put it back in my pocket, mostly because I was a bit embarrassed, I pretended that I had meant to do it. At the next session another person mentioned it and another conversation ensued.

This principle works whether it's wearing a Tough Mudder t-shirt, a button with a funny saying or using a pen to make a bun out of your hair (not something I've done but I've commented on it to other people).

Because of my intense involvement in local BBBS agencies, I was asked to join the National Board of Directors, once again, being thrust into a new, uncomfortable situation. I still remember that first board meeting on Friday afternoon where I said nothing other than introducing myself.

A few months later, at the next meeting in Edmonton, I was very nervous and intent on not screwing up. My default is to sit back and listen quietly, but I knew that wouldn't make a great first impression, nor was it why I was asked to join the board. But speaking boldly and loudly isn't my nature either.

So I decided to take the middle road. I used my introvert skills to listen intently and was careful to only speak when I had a strong opinion or was knowledgeable about something regarding local agencies. I think in the first weekend, in the over twelve hours of meetings, I probably only shared my thoughts three or four times.

And I really focused my attention during the breaks and down times. I spent lots of time visiting with other board members and asking them lots of questions. Sometimes, speaking up isn't the easiest thing to do so this is another strategy that an introvert can use to become known and be part of the group without having to be the boisterous one.

It's at these types of events that I re-learn a major truth in life – most people know a heck of a lot about stuff that I don't. Their life experiences make them very smart and perceptive in their own way. So, I try to spend way more time listening and learning. It goes back to the adage that we were given two ears and one mouth for a reason.

To this day, I still do the same thing. I've gotten more comfortable in my role on the board as a representative of small, local agencies. I also haven't changed my approach very much either – trying to speak only when I feel that I have something important to add.

My work on the National Board for BBBS has also pushed me one step further in my public speaking. Part of my role on the board is the requirement to get up in front of 300 people at a conference and introduce a speaker or give an award. This past summer, it moved another step when I read a speech in both French and English. Once again I was amazed at the grace we have for our fellow humans. I'm sure I butchered the French but people said that I did really well.

I met Vy Tri almost as soon as I moved to BC eleven years ago. He was organizing a weekly Ultimate Frisbee game, a sport that I started playing in Edmonton. Right away, you could tell that Vy Tri was an extrovert – he talked to everyone, was assertive, and ran the show. He made new people feel comfortable. It was really easy to get to know him.

Change is possible.

As our friendship grew, having kids at the same time, playing hockey, and just visiting, I still didn't see the introverted side of him, other than knowing that he spent a lot of time at home tinkering with computer stuff.

When he brought up the idea of this book and that he was a closet introvert too, I wasn't shocked. He's just like many people I know. If you were to look around in most workplaces, community groups, or social settings, it seems that the majority of people are extroverts, because extroversion is the type of personality that is called for at in those situations.

But we know that half of the population leans towards introversion. Even now, only the people that really know me well know that I'm an introvert.

To me, this book is about two things. First, being comfortable with who you are. Being an introvert is a good thing. It is who you are so you should embrace it. We will show you the qualities of introversion that make you a great person.

Second, in many social and business settings, the qualities of extroversion work better. It will make your business or organization more successful. When advocating for your kids or a favourite charity, being heard can be more effective. And it's a skill set that can be learned as both Vy Tri and I can attest.

Learning to be an extrovert takes work – a lot of work – but I can promise you that it will be worthwhile.

Vy Tri's Story

My ambivert journey started in high school when I made my first conscious decision to change. And that journey continues even today, though it's more of a refinement these days.

As many studies show, introversion and extroversion aren't like two sides of a coin. They're on a continuum. And for me, it's been a long daily journey along that continuum.

What I clearly remember, though, is the day when someone remarked that they wished they were as extroverted as me. It was a sunny day in South Surrey, BC, circa summer 2010. The person doing the remarking was our admin/receptionist, Carrie. (Not her real name.)

I was an independent mortgage broker with a leading mortgage franchise. Incidentally, this is probably one of the more extroverted careers you can pursue, right after real estate agent and politician. So if you find yourself in one of these careers and are exhausted mentally, now you know why.

Introversion and extroversion aren't like two sides of a coin. They're on a continuum.

Carrie was talking about how she wanted to become a broker as well, but couldn't because of what she felt was her "fatal flaw." According to Carrie, she was smarter than some of the brokers in the office, but couldn't talk as well and wasn't as charming. This was a people-business and she wasn't a people-person. She really wished she was, but it just wasn't in her nature. Not like Vy Tri. Noooo, Vy Tri was so naturally comfortable and good-humoured with people.

My first thought was "Huh? Who are you talking about?" After realizing that it was me, I informed Carrie that I was not a natural. In fact, I worked very hard at it so that it would seem like I was a natural. This revelation, of course, floored Carrie.

Like many others, Carrie failed to see the hard work that goes into looking natural or talented at something. Many times, when something looks natural, chances are that person put a lot of blood, sweat, and tears into it. For me, it took years and years of focused effort. Many of those years were of the "fake it till you make it" kind.

Carrie had assumed that I was just a natural. You could see the look of incomprehension in her eyes. It was not a subtle gesture. Of course, I was floored myself. Had I arrived? Had I truly become that outgoing person I'd wanted to be in donkey's years? (For all you non-Irish folk that means an indeterminable time frame.) Later that week, I posted this event on Facebook and, yes, there were plenty of people who thought I was an extrovert. This was CRAZY! Up until that point in my life, I never would have considered that was how the world viewed me.

Then, being an introvert, I decided to analyze myself. As it turns out, I was not the person I thought I was in my mind. Ever since I graduated high school and attended university, I'd always strived to be extroverted. But in my head, I had never made it. Every year I would try to be more outgoing, more sociable, more of a people person. And every year, I would chalk up a loss, a failure. It never occurred to me that I was actually making progress. You know those squiggly stock market charts where the general trend is up? That's what was happening, and I didn't even know it.

I had subscribed to the black or white, introvert or extrovert theory. The concept of a personality continuum wasn't around back then. Or maybe it was, but I was too busy inside my own head to have noticed. After so many years of recording the same failures in my mind, I never considered taking another look at the scoreboard. I never considered that I had actually accomplished my goal.

Talking to people nowadays doesn't seem to be a problem for me. In fact, I quite enjoy it. Small talk is easy. Ditto talking to strangers. Add to that a resounding "yes" to sales. My most recent three jobs were in sales.

Upon reflection, I learned three important lessons:

1. Becoming extroverted is a skill.
2. Any skill can be acquired.
3. Anyone can develop the traits they desire with enough practice and perseverance.

Think about that for a second. Being outgoing and sociable are skills, and skills can be learned. Any talent you desire can be learned if you're stubborn enough to stick to it. There are best-selling books based solely on this premise. Most notably are *The Talent Code: Greatness Isn't Born. It's Grown. Here's How* by Daniel Coyle and *Talent Is Overrated: What Really Separates World-Class Performers from Everybody Else* by Geoff Colvin.

In fact, my kids attend a karate school where they have a saying written on the wall:

> A black belt is a white belt who did not quit.

That should be enough to empower you to break out of your shell and move forward. What's your version of being a black belt? Is it being able to talk about anything with anyone? Is it being able to connect with people who were complete strangers a moment ago? Is it to effectively present ideas and sway others to your point of view?

As we'll see in later chapters, what your version of ambivert looks like is really up to you. Use the shopping cart method to customize ambivert to your liking.

Whatever you desire, you have to start and keep going. Never quit. In order to persevere, you have to have a really big reason to embark on the journey. I had an inner desire and a vision of what I wanted to be.

Your version of Ambiversion is up to you.

Perhaps it was hormones, but I remember that desire to gain friends and be popular being very strong. I was a shy nerd and I wanted to be an outgoing people-person. That want turned into a need for me. And that's the key to this journey.

You really have to want to do it. Why? Because it is hard. Some would say, "stupid-hard." I did a lot of soul searching during the early years. I spent a lot of time in my own head wondering what the hell was the matter with me. I will admit that I cried sometimes. Everyone else seemed to be able to make friends easily, and they didn't seem like they had to fake their enthusiasm.

Now, as a kid, in the 1980's and 1990's, there wasn't a written manual that said, "If you want to be more outgoing, do steps 1, 2, and 3." So, like many of you out there, I had to figure this out on my own.

Two events helped me break through the mental barrier of merely wanting to be more outgoing to actually taking the first step in doing so.

First, in the summer of 1995, my parents and I decided it would be a good idea for me to learn Mandarin Chinese. We had tried some private schooling but my development was quite limited without anyone to converse with. So, we decided that I would go to a Chinese language camp for 3 weeks. The "camp" was held at a university in Vancouver, BC.

Each kid got a room and stayed in the residences. Each one of us from Canada was paired with a kid from China or Taiwan. Yes, someone flew halfway around the world to be my language partner for 3 weeks. Poor kid.

The idea was for us to learn from each other since we would be inseparable for that time. My buddy was an extremely shy guy with big glasses who didn't exercise very much. After looking at the buddies everyone else got, I groaned. I didn't have to spend ALL my time with him did I? So I ditched my language partner and spent a lot of time with the Canadians and their cooler buddies. Kids are so mean. But I was on a mission. This was my first time away from home (ever) and I wanted to make the most of the experience. No one here knew I was a geek, so it was an opportunity to start on the "cool" side.

Yes, I really thought it would work out like that.

My buddy was quite content to stay in his group of friends as well. So win-win. The teachers didn't like that so much, so when they were around, we kinda had to stick together.

During the camp, we basically toured all of Vancouver and Victoria for three weeks. I didn't learn very much when it came to improving my Chinese language skills. But I did "come out of my shell" during that time. When my parents picked me up, they said I had changed. I wouldn't stop talking.

Overall, it was a blast and I really owe a lot of my development to that camp. But I cringe when I think back to that time. Hindsight is always 20/20, and boy was I an uncontrollable fool. While I thought I was being cool, I was actually being a "weirdovert." My level of excitement was all wrong; it was too extreme at the wrong times. My spontaneity came across as controlling/demanding. I was voted "most likely to be a camp teacher." I purchased a traditional Kung Fu outfit and wore it everywhere, thinking I was so cool. Looking at the pictures now, it looked like I wore pyjamas the whole time. My most embarrassing moment came during the send-off party. I couldn't dance but I tried anyways. It was weird and awkward. I was definitely not cool. Now, I didn't know all these things at the time, so I had a blast.

While I credit this experience with being one of the big mile-markers of my life, it is an ugly one.

My second big break through event happened the following school year. I got the opportunity to go on a one-week trip to Ottawa, ON. Kids from across the country came together in the nation's capital in order to learn more about kids from other parts of the country.

All the boys bunked (literally) in the same room and all the girls in their room. I was extremely uncomfortable. I had to sleep with everyone else and live out of a suitcase under my bed. The worst part was the toilets which were all stalls, public washroom style. And you had to cross the toilets to get to the showers. Not cool. It was the first time in my life where I couldn't escape somewhere for privacy.

It was an extremely extroverted environment. However, without any other choice, I adapted. Every thing was done in groups. In a weird logic-twist, I thanked God for that. Now all the cool kids were forced to hang out with me.

We visited Parliament. It was a fantastic experience. I experienced an Ottawa classic: eating Beaver Tails while ice-skating on the Rideau Canal. Also very cool. Literally in this case. I think I was minutes away from hypothermia since all my clothes were designed for British Columbia weather.

For the last night, we had to create a skit that encapsulated what each of our provinces were all about. The only thing I remember is the Saskatchewan girls thrusting out their chests and saying "it ain't all flat in the prairies." So shoot me, I was a teenage boy.

There was a dance at the end as well. Now, I learned my lesson from the language camp, and didn't even approach the dance floor. I hung out either outside, or by the snack table. Then a girl from Quebec came to find me. She said something in French that I didn't understand and it was obvious she wanted to dance with me. I didn't want to dance period. Plus she was weird and kinda creepy, so double period. But she kept pouring her heart out to me "en Français" so I eventually relented. It was the most awkward side-stepping-in-a-circle moment ever. Now I knew how those girls at the language camp felt when I asked them to dance. Karma will always find you. Anyways, that girl is probably a cover model now.

Where was I going with this story? Right. Comfort zones. Both of these events forced me well outside of my comfort zone. I really grew as a person and learned a lot of valuable social skills. The key in both cases was to change my environment and completely immerse myself in it. You are a product of your environment; so if you want to change, start with changing your surroundings. Different input and different stimuli will usually lead to different results.

Growth begins at the edge of your comfort zone.

That is the only logical way to explain what happened next. After high school, I decided I would do my post-secondary education some place I've never been and where I knew no one. Basically hit the reset button on my life.

And reset it was. In fact, I punched right through the damn button.

As we saw in Edwin's story, "reset" is a common theme amongst introverts who need to change. Edwin moved from Albert to BC in order to reset. I went to from the mainland to Vancouver Island.

Somehow, we knew instinctively that we had to change our surroundings and influences. So many introverts will move far away in order to start a new life where no one knows our "little secret." In these new places, we have more freedom to try new things. No one is going to make fun of us if they don't know us. So, in a sense it's safer. When Edwin first started traveling for Big Brothers Big Sisters, he was put in a new environment, and felt he had the freedom to try new things and be more outgoing. It's worked out nicely for him.

The idea of "reset" does work, but beware the law of unintended consequences. There is one very significant downside: when we move, we also lose our support network.

It caused my journey to be 100x harder. My university days were a confusing mess. More than once I regretted not staying close to home and going to school with everyone else from my grad class. It was a lonely time and I threw some epic pity parties for myself. I definitely did not have the tools to make friends easily. I thought I did after going through those adventures the last two years of high school, but I was woefully unprepared.

I was a weirdovert at this stage. Stuck somewhere between introversion and what I thought was extroversion. And no one wants to be around a weirdo. Making friends as a weirdovert is harder than making friends as an introvert. It was a real lesson in social dynamics.

University is a microcosm of the real world. Everyone is trying to make their own way through life. They have their own career paths, extra-curricular activities, and social groups. Making it into someone's circle requires certain social skills. I will say this about university: while I did get book smart, I became really street smart by the time I graduated.

However, I didn't learn it all on my own. Actually, I learned virtually none of it on my own. My development really began with me getting into Amway. Yes, those multi-level-network-marketing folks we all know and love. I'm serious about this. Everyone "high-up" in Amway that I've ever interacted with was a professional businessperson through and through. I read about the same nonsense that's on the Internet about them, and I have yet to see it for myself. I don't necessarily agree with everything going on there, and I'm no longer a part of Amway, but I respect the men and women who are in it and who continue to build towards their own dreams.

What Amway did for me was give me a vision for the future and a goal to work towards. We talked earlier about giving yourself a huge goal and a huge reason to change. You will not pull yourself out of bed at zero-dark-thirty without that motivation. You need a goal to force yourself to work on the difficult and uncomfortable rather than veg-out on the couch.

Amway gave me that goal. Or rather, they showed me how to set my own goals and gave me the tools to achieve them. Through their system, I discovered that one of the keys to any sort of paradigm shift in your life is mentorship.

Enter Andy Stewart. Andy became my mentor for three key years of my life. I owe him and his wife Anita so much for my development. As I look back now, I wonder what Andy was thinking when he agreed to take me under his wing. I wasn't pretty when I started.

We talked almost daily. He taught me the fundamentals of people skills. He taught me the nuances of human interaction. He taught me to dig deep and focus on the goal when things didn't go right. And he did all of this for free. He wouldn't even allow me to buy his coffee (tall Americano with room, in case you wanted to know). Here's a tip of the hat to you, Andy and Anita.

I've taken that attitude of paying it forward with me ever since. Everywhere I go, I try to add value to people's lives. Leave everyone a little better off when I leave.

Focusing on others helps you be more outgoing.

We'll get into this concept on this in later chapters, but one of the mental tricks to help you become more outgoing is to focus on others. If you concentrate on bringing a smile to someone's face, giving them a tip for a problem they are working on, or simply sharing something you think they may enjoy, it will make your ambivert journey easier.

When you add value to people's lives, they will like you. When they like you, they will communicate with you and listen to what you have to say. And that's how you start to develop a reputation and expand your sphere of influence.

By focusing on helping others, you will inevitably help yourself. This is another one of those ironic principles the universe loves to dish out.

Anyways, after university, I took some time off personal development. Not voluntarily, but life just happened. Getting a job, finding a girl, and getting married will do that.

After a few failed career choices, I decided to pursue my Rich Dad Poor Dad dreams in real estate. But I was too afraid of people to become a real estate agent. So, in a moment of cognitive brilliance, I decided to become a mortgage broker instead.

W.T.F.

As I mentioned earlier, if you're an introvert and you've tried that business, you understand. Capital W, capital T, capital F. Needless to say, I slowly got out of that and went to work at a bank in a job with a salary.

When I look back, I often wonder if I had any regrets about my journey. You bet I do. Knowing what I know now, I would have changed practically everything I did. But woulda, coulda, shoulda, right? There's no point in wishing to change the past. Life's scars are what make up the beautiful tapestry that is you.

Over time, Edwin and I have learned to bear our scars proudly. We've learned that doing so makes us relatable which in turn adds to our self-confidence. As we'll see in the following chapters, relatability and self-confidence are keys to being an ambivert.

Life's scars are what make up the beautiful tapestry that is you.

We've shared our stories to give you hope. In my case, it should give you a lot of hope. With any luck, you can relate to some of our experiences, take some of our wisdom (I use that term loosely) and shortcut some of your own painful years.

The coming chapters will focus on applying these lessons to help you create your own changes. Chief amongst those lessons is learning what to shoot for. Being an extrovert shouldn't be the goal. In fact, it could lead your further away from your goal. Instead, introverts should focus on becoming an ambivert: the ideal middle ground. As you'll see in the next chapter, ambiverts have their own unique set of advantages.

The Ambivert Advantage

By Edwin

We have all heard the terms introvert and extrovert, but what do they mean? Most commonly, people think introvert is synonymous with shy, quiet, bookish; sitting in a library studying or programming a computer. Extroverts are sociable, loud, outgoing – the crazies who are the life of the party.

Pop culture tells us that the qualities of extroversion are more valued. Movies are filled with outgoing protagonists. Political leaders are voted in based on popularity, which often depends on being a good public speaker. The leader of a sports team is usually the vocal person who is encouraging their teammates to greater heights. The promoted employee is the one who stands out.

But what if the better leader is the more thoughtful, quieter type? What if the best politician is the one who can make good decisions under pressure rather than the one with the biggest smile and the firmest handshake? What if the best captain for the team is the one who leads by example, working hard and offering a private piece of advice here and there?

Obviously, by picking up this book, you think you are an introvert (or maybe you are wanting to learn about your spouse, friend, or co-worker). You are likely looking for some advice on how to become better at something, whether that is being in public, leading, or selling.

So first, before we talk about how to change, let's learn what introversion, extroversion, and ambiversion really are.

Introversion and extroversion are just two ends of a long continuum with ambiversion in the middle. Each of us fall somewhere on the line. We are born leaning to one side or the other and our life experiences move us along the continuum. There is no right or wrong to where you are on this line. And there is no perfect place to be on this line. But knowing where you are on the continuum will help you in your interactions with others and your success in life.

Our favourite description of introversion/extroversion centers on one's response to stimuli (or where you get your energy from).

Introverts prefer fewer stimuli. They get their energy when there is one, strong source of stimuli such as reading a book or talking to one or two people at a time. They like to be able to focus on one thing at a time. In contrast, extroverts thrive when there are much more stimuli. They want many things to be happening at once. They want to be where the action is.

Let's start with an oversimplification: if you think of a party, the extrovert is in the middle of the dance floor, having a yelling conversation with another dancer while waving to their friend who is across the room. The introvert is sitting by the bar, talking to one person.

Half of us are introverts

Vy Tri and I are examples of ambiverts with introvert tendencies. We love to be in the middle of things for a period of time, but then, it's off to the side where we can get away from the noise. We get an initial charge with being in a place with a lot of stimuli, but staying there eventually becomes a drain and an effort. We are more introverted than extroverted, but that doesn't mean we never want to be in the middle of a wild and crazy time.

Half of the population falls into the introvert category – so we are not alone. However, in many settings (school, work, parties) being an extrovert seems preferable, so many introverts have learned to fake it, leading to the misconception that introverts are a minority. You may be surprised to learn that these people were and are introverts too: Abraham Lincoln, Eleanor Roosevelt, Christina Aguilera, Courtney Cox, and Roy Rodgers. Each of these people was or is a successful public speaker and an icon to thousands of people.

The reason we are writing a book is that we believe it's great to be an introvert. We feel that introverts do some things better than extroverts. Introverts:

- are more introspective and analytical about what's going on around them.
- pick up on social cues quicker.
- function better than extroverts when tired.
- learn more quickly from mistakes.
- are more empathetic.
- like talking about weightier issues.
- are more patient.
- have more perseverance.
- do better in college (though they have similar IQs to extroverts).
- are better at delaying gratification.

However, there are many things that extroverts do better. Extroverts:

- create better first impressions.
- have less inhibitions with what they say.
- are less self-critical.
- are better at filling in the awkward silences.

- lighten the mood better.
- do better in elementary school.
- are more relaxed.
- are more comfortable public speakers.
- are better at being the glue that holds groups of people together.
- are quicker to express their opinions.
- are more likely to be chosen as leaders.
- are listened to more often (mostly because introverts aren't talking).

This book is about learning to embrace the things we are naturally good at and then learn those things that will make us more successful in situations where extroversion works better.

Extroverts can teach us three main things:

1. First impressions matter.
2. People want to connect with you.
3. The world isn't as scary as you think.

Let's examine each of these one at a time, starting with first impressions. Talkative people are commonly rated as smarter, better looking, more interesting and more desirable as friends. They are more likely to be chosen as the leader of a group. Their opinions are given more weight. Study after study shows that the first impression does more to influence what people think of you than anything else that comes after.

We are not saying that you need to be the most talkative person around. But being the quietest is a bad place to start. Thankfully, in the long run, people will value substance over style so a talkative person with terrible ideas will eventually get found out. But don't lose the race right out of the gate. Work to be respected in the beginning because you are not a wallflower and then use your natural abilities to analyze, process and communicate clearly.

The second thing we learn from extroverts is how to more easily connect with others. Humans are wired to be social. People with more connections are more successful, are happier, are healthier, get more done and make a bigger difference. But it is sometimes difficult to make those connections.

In a conversation, when a person throws out potential connection points (things we might have in common with them) grab onto those that apply to you. In a matter of minutes, you will hear about family situations, jobs, their day, and a few other stories. Extroverts are great at throwing out connection points and recognizing them in others, thus creating the opportunity to keep the conversation flowing. This makes you feel more connected to them, which leads to more interactions. Vy Tri will elaborate on this in the Small Talk chapter.

Finally extroverts teach us that the world is not as scary as you think. Extroverts are constantly embarrassing themselves with their need to fill dead air. They throw out so much stuff that some of it is terrible and/or awkward. It doesn't faze them because they've learned to quickly move on to something else.

I was thinking about this at a recent party where I carefully watched an extrovert at work. Because he was so comfortable at constantly throwing stuff at the room, we just kept laughing, even when his material didn't fit or failed to connect (first impressions matter). We loved to be around him because he was able to fill in the silences and keep us entertained (connecting with others). He made it much less work for us and because we knew it, we were willing to give him a long leash (the world isn't scary). We remember and emphasize the good stuff because we would rather have an extrovert fill in the dead air than have to do it ourselves.

Embrace your introversion.

We are going to talk about the specific skills to become more ambiverted in the next chapter, but before you leave this one, we want to remind you of a few things.

Being an introvert is who you are and it's something that people will value over time. As you read in our stories, both of us embrace our introversion. It helps makes us better at our jobs. I remember a conversation with a therapist who said that the quality that makes people like us is also the quality that we will struggle with. Because I'm very analytical, thoughtful, and deep thinking, I'm sometimes not the most fun person to be around. But if I tried to change that – by becoming louder and crazier, the very thing that people love and respect about me might disappear.

Being an introvert is something you can't change. When you think about the introversion spectrum, you can move along it a little bit, but you won't be able to get to the other end of the line. And that is okay. In fact, it's great because you're not a weirdovert (more on that later). But it also means that you don't have to be an introvert in all settings. Your challenge will be in learning where and when being an extrovert is a good thing and how to do it.

Being an introvert does not mean you are alone. Half of the world's population are introverts. We just keep it hidden a bit more. Remember, people want to connect and the world isn't as scary as we think.

When I'm at parties, I can always find someone who is also looking to have a quiet conversation. In many cases, they are looking for an out and I can provide that for them. At times, I've gone off to a corner to read, fallen asleep on the couch, or taken my kids for a walk. I've admitted this to people and rather than getting ridiculed, they confess to me that they've snuck upstairs for a quick nap or took a turn hiding somewhere else too (the bathroom is a common place). Don't be scared to be honest with your friends. Studies show that everyone likes to be truly known and I've found that others are more accepting and kinder than I would expect.

Being an introvert means you need to revert to your default at times to recharge. We would be the last people to suggest that you need to be an extrovert all the time. Vy Tri and I take our introvert time very seriously, whether it's exercising, programming, reading, or having one on one quiet conversations. Each activity helps us to recharge so that when we need to be more outgoing, we have the energy to do so.

So enjoy the journey. We all have the capacity to be more than just who we are today. So if you are moving in circles where extroversion would help, then do it. Learn from it. Embrace it. Be challenged by it.

This is the only life you get to live. If you aren't happy today, then why do you think it will be better tomorrow? To quote an old saying, *"If ten coins are not enough to make a man rich, what if you add one coin? What if you add another? Finally, you will have to say that no one can be rich unless one coin can make him so."* So if you are not happy today, tomorrow isn't likely to be much different.

Vy Tri's Thoughts

In North America, you virtually have to be outgoing to make it. Edwin has been self-employed most of his life, and he needed to change in order to succeed. I've been climbing the corporate ladder, and I definitely can say that you have to be seen as competent and charismatic to be promoted. As Edwin said, our society is obsessed with extroverts.

It seems that there are so many more extroverts than introverts out there. However, that is because many of us introverts recognized the bias in society, adapted and became ambiverts. When you look at an ambivert, on the surface, they are virtually indistinguishable from an extrovert. And that's the whole point. It's not until you dig deep that you find the more serious contemplative side.

As we can see from Edwin's list of true introverts who we think are extroverts, they have mastered being ambiverts.

To take Edwin's point one step further. I would say that being an introvert is awesome, but we can enhance those advantages by incorporating some extroverted traits. For example, introverts are analytical and empathetic. We can enhance that by incorporating a public speaking ability. The result is we can convey meaningful ideas, persuade people to our line of thinking, and create change in the world.

That's why we call it the ambivert advantage. It's introversion being enhanced by extroversion.

You will never ever become a true extrovert. Never. The more you try the weirder you get.

Going too far though is not good. You still need to stay true to yourself. That may sound a bit contradictory, but here's where many introverts like myself have messed up. Since you were born an introvert, you will never, ever become a true extrovert. Never. The more you try the weirder you get.

As you'll see in the next chapter, introverts who try too hard to be extroverted often lack the finesse that true extroverts have. The result is actions or speech that is too extreme and that doesn't seem quite right. They are weird. (We call them weirdoverts.)

So you need to work with your strengths. Don't shun your quiet, reflective nature. In fact, nurture those qualities because that's your gift. But at the same time, strategically adapt some extroverted traits so that you have a nice balance in your life. Edwin and I have found that over time, we really value the extroverted traits we picked up. They have become a fundamental part of who we are. But we always make sure we go back and do the things that recharge and renew us. I hope that makes sense. Being an ambivert is hard work because you must master two personality types.

Weirdoverts

By Vy Tri

We coined the term "weirdovert" in the last chapter, so now we better define it:

> weir-do-vert *[weer-doe-vert]*
>
> 1. An introvert who acts in an extremely loud or excited manner thinking that he/she is being extroverted;
>
> 2. Forced or false spontaneity that just looks weird;
>
> 3. Not how an extrovert would actually act: *she was being a weirdovert in her celebrations.*

Edwin and I chose the term "Weirdovert" because it adequately and humorously encompasses the stage of life that introverts inevitably grow through. If you've become an ambivert, chances are you've spent some time in weirdovert-land.

An introvert can never become an extrovert; it is an unattainable goal. Extroversion is your natural asymptote; it's a boundary you can never truly reach. The more you try to approach it, the weirder you get. For you scientists, it's like trying to accelerate a ship to the speed of light. It requires exponentially more energy to move the ship as it's speed increases.

This is the same as an introvert's required energy output as they approach extroversion. That extra energy required makes turns them weird.

The typical process goes introvert to awkwardvert then jumps to weirdovert and finally backs off to ambivert as you refine your behaviour.

The Journey to Ambiversion

©2015 Edwin Palsma
& Vy Tri Truong

This process bears a little more explanation. As the illustration above shows, we all start out as introverts spending at lot of time in our own heads. Then at some point we make the decision that we want to come out of our shell and become more outgoing. We begin by taking the first few tentative steps, which we call the awkwardvert stage. This is actually not too bad. We are trying new things and people are generally accepting of our efforts. In fact, they probably compliment us and encourage us. We will do things that are embarrassing, but those moments are usually easy to recover from. Easy baby steps, nothing too crazy. It would be ideal if we could spend more time in this stage, refine our behaviours slowly and then make a nice seamless transition to ambiversion.

Sadly, the awkwardvert stage usually doesn't last long enough for that to occur. Here's why: as we get used to being more "out there" we start to take more chances with our behaviour. Once we realize that we can be more than we are and can live outside our own heads, that knowledge and freedom becomes intoxicating. Literally. Do you remember when you first tried a glass of wine? It was good. So you had another glass. And it was even better. Soon, you've had way too much to drink and you start acting a little funny. Extroversion can have that exact same effect on introverts.

It's like we become addicted to extroversion. As a result of this behavioural bingeing, we end up skipping ambiversion all together and jump directly to the weirdovert stage. It is both an over-zealous reaction to a newfound freedom and also a by-product of our own ignorance. As introverts first coming out of our shell, we don't realize that we can't actually become full-fledged extroverts. When we try, we push ourselves too far and become weirdoverts.

Weirdoverts are rude, obnoxious, and loud. They try to copy extroverts by turning off the filter between their brain and their mouth. The problem is while extroverts have a generally fun-loving, slapstick, Forest Gump view of the world, introverts have a patronizing, cynical, Debbie Downer view of the world. The result is when extroverts turn off their filter, what comes out might be stupid but it is in a funny or innocent sort of way. When an introvert does it, it sounds like whining. Example:

Extrovert: "I went on a wine tour and they told us to spit out the wine and not swallow. I didn't listen and wow, I got drunk fast!"

Weirdovert: "They wanted us to taste the wine and then spit it out. That's ridiculous. I paid a lot of money for this tour. Besides they have a bus that takes us around. I'm not sure what their problem is!"

The volume also tends to be much louder in weirdoverts. Any celebration is more flamboyant and bigger than is required. The obnoxiously loud one in the group is the weirdovert: "Oh YEAH! That's a great idea! Let's DO THAT!!" There's probably some arm waving and pointing in there as well.

Weirdoverts also don't know when not to talk to you. I was at a café with a client and there were only the two of us there. We were having a conversation about different coffees around the world. During our conversation, the person sweeping the floor on the other side of the café yells, "are you talking about us?" I said "no," and gave a brief explanation. Then I turned back to the client to continue where we left off. But the floor sweeper kept talking to us. From across the room!

So how do you know if you're a weirdovert yourself? That's part of the problem. You often don't know while you're in that stage. It's often hard to see the forest for the trees.

It's incredibly similar to boiling a frog: turn up the temperature of the water gradually so that the frog doesn't realize it's boiling.

The other problem is no one will actually tell you that you're weird. They just won't invite you out very often or they are always busy when you want to hang out.

Another challenge is realizing that there is such a thing as a weirdovert. For some of you, it will click right away. You know exactly who weirdoverts are, you've just been waiting for a definition. For some others, it might be more helpful to point out the nuances.

To illustrate, let's take the popular sitcom Friends. It ran for ten years, so chances are you are at least vaguely familiar with it. Joey is the classic extrovert. Confident, outgoing, and generally fun-loving. Chandler is an ambivert. He is thoughtful, sometimes-tongue-tied, and sarcastic. But he is also sociable and funny. Ross is... Ross. He's a weirdovert. He flirts with his cousin and has a pet monkey. In the episode where they are moving the couch, he yells "Pivot! Piiiivooootttt!" Classic weirdovert behaviour. Watch a few episodes to see more examples.

Probably the best sitcom just full of weirdoverts is *The Office*. The boss, Michael Scott, is a rare example of an extrovert trying very hard to be introverted. Andy Bernard is a weirdovert, yet oddly relatable. The Dwight Schrute character is an extreme weirdovert. I actually once worked with a guy that must've been 50% Dwight.

Here's a comparison table to help you out at your office:

Situation	Weirdovert	Extrovert
Acknowledge a win in an office contest	Waives arms above head, shouts "wooooo!"	Fist pump, smiles. Makes a funny joke
Making a joke about someone or something	Sounds critical with condescending overtones	Makes joke
Meeting new people	Leads off with deep discussion on world events	"What's up?" or "How's it going, eh?"
Small talk	Talks about themselves while whining about something	Laughs, smiles, says something that allows you to jump in
Sales	Sells by being critical of the competition	Promotes the benefits of their product or service

So how does weirdoversion develop? Well, it starts as we travel on our continuum towards extroversion. We discover that the world did not shun us or laugh at us, and we start to gain self-confidence. We have to be careful as this self-confidence can develop into an attitude of not giving a damn about what people think.

This often comes across as cockiness. Remember Edwin's story. He started to become bold and used that attitude to try and fit in. Something went wrong and it came across at taking jabs at people. In weirdoverts, this cockiness isn't them lifting themselves up as much as it is putting everyone else down. This is an important distinction as an extrovert will provide positive energy but the weirdovert will convey negative energy. Example:

Extrovert: "Yeah, I can get that done."

Weirdovert: "Sit down guys. Better let me handle this."

Talking down to others, being critical or condescending, using offensive language, or making aggressive assertions are all cocky ways in which weirdoverts act. It's like taking power versus earning power. It doesn't matter whether or not they do this with any malicious intent; this is how it comes across.

In extroverts, you can sense the self-confidence. It permeates through everything they are from the way they conduct themselves to their dress and their mannerisms. In weirdoverts you see a bit of a smirk on their face and everything is just a bit off. It's like when someone types up a list and uses spaces instead of tabs: nothing quite lines up perfectly.

Once, I was on the same beer league hockey team as a weirdovert. He was never in the right position, constantly gave the puck away, and got in the way of his teammates. But in the dressing room, he always thought he played well. He thought he just missed a couple of chances and almost setup a couple of goals. The fact that he caused us to lose did not even cross his mind. The loss was chalked up to bad luck. He still compares himself to his buddies who played major junior. He's in his 50's, and I'm not sure he'll ever figure things out.

In all honesty, my life was headed down that same path. I'm so fortunate that I came across Amway, and more specifically, Andy Stewart's intervention. Even so, it took me a long time to figure out the correct behaviours. I thought much of the criticism was unwarranted and unfair at the time. I disagreed with many of the suggestions thrown my way. I'll be honest, it was my ego that wouldn't let the truth into my head. Any perceived chink in my new armour was greeted with denials. I think this is the same ailment that affected my hockey buddy.

As we talked about earlier: while I was being a weirdovert, I didn't know that I was being a weirdovert. In my own mind, I was being extroverted. I was being loud, I was acting out, I was spontaneous, and I was doing all the things I THOUGHT extroverts did. The fact that I was being annoying did not even occur to me and even when it did, I didn't care. I was getting the attention I'd been craving and I loved it! This newfound freedom was exhilarating. Anyone who told me otherwise could go to hell as far as I was concerned.

Looking back, I see that I was an uncontrollable fool for many years. I gained new friends but lost them just as quickly. My stubbornness in not stepping back and evaluating my behaviour prolonged the weirdovert stage. So, to everyone who tried to help me out: sorry about that.

After years of repeatedly being told to tone it down, I finally started to listen. I wanted different results in my life and was ready to be a student.

I became heavily devoted to personal development. I can't emphasize this enough. If you are a weirdovert or think you may be, you would be wise to start a program like this as well. I've heard it described as flattening out the peaks and valleys of life's events. The events are the same, but your reactions are less extreme.

Quiet self-confidence is a key to ambiversion.

Through books and seminars, my cocky confidence slowly settled into a quiet confidence. I learned that I didn't need to put others down in order to shine. We could all be great together. I came to realize that everyone was my superior in some way or form. With this quiet confidence, I was finally at a stage in my life where I could back off the throttle and start to settle into true ambiversion.

As we will explore in the following chapters, quiet self-confidence is the base you need to build on in order to achieve ambiversion. A lot of weirdoverts act cocky because they actually lack true self-confidence. They are faking it even if they are not aware they are doing it.

Some weirdoverts just plain don't know any better. They think they are awesome and are doing the right things. They have an innocent child-like confidence borne of ignorance. They have absolutely no idea how others really see them. Honestly, some people are just that clueless. You probably know a few.

I had another buddy who went on over 50 first dates in less than a year. That's torrid pace for any playboy. However, this buddy wasn't a playboy. He just messed up the first date so many times that there usually wasn't a second date. You have to be immensely talented to not get a girl with that many tries. Even if just by accident. However, if you knew my buddy, he has a knack for showing you two things: First is how cheap he is. The guy even brings his own Tupperware containers to dinner parties and office luncheons. Let that one sink in for a minute. So you can imagine who pays on the dates. The second thing is he tends to talk forever about what's on his mind regardless of the relevancy. It's like he's having an independent conversation to the one you're having.

I like to label my buddy as being "situationally-unaware." It happens because he is so completely inward focused. He is only thinking about himself. His brain is likely running these thoughts: How is the world treating me today? How have I done today? How does everything affect me? He is oblivious to the needs, wants, and situations of the people around him.

Weirdoverts are notoriously situationally-unaware. They need to learn to take their eyes off themselves and see the world beyond their own nose. This is an essential skill in becoming an ambivert. It's not easy because introverts are, by definition, inward focused.

Once upon a time, I had a co-worker who was always late for everything. It was like he had no concept of time. The problem was our boss was all about being on-time. This was her number one requirement. If there was a meeting, you were expected to be there on-time. To her, being on-time is all about respecting the people with whom that commitment has been made. So my tardy co-worker was always in her bad books. Then he would complain indignantly about our boss. It never occurred to him that he was causing his own misery. He needed to develop an awareness for the situation at hand. My co-worker needed to think about the other stakeholders and what they wanted.

Being a recovering weirdovert, I also had to develop situational awareness. Luckily, I had some friends point it out to me in the way only buddies can: by fake-slapping me every time it occurred. I didn't realize that I was being such a dork. The concept of situational-awareness didn't exist in my head before then. It was an eye-opener.

So how do you develop situational-awareness? For one, you can get someone to fake-slap you each time. Or, perhaps less embarrassing, you start by using your number one asset: your brain. Think about the people involved in the situation and ask yourself some variation of the following:

- What are their motivations?
- What do they want to accomplish?
- What is going on in their lives that might impact the situation?
- If I were them, how would I react if I did A, B, or C?
- Would that result be beneficial? If not, how can I adjust what I'm doing?
- How can I add value to them during this interaction?

Notice how none of these questions have anything to do with what you want. That's because what you want comes second. Identify what everyone else wants first and then see how you can help them towards that. Then you can get to work on what you want. People are more willing to help you if you help them first. It's one of the basic rules of human psychology and one of the first lessons in any success book.

You don't have to sit down for fifteen minutes and think through all those questions in detail for every situation. Use your intuition, make jumps in logic, extrapolate. You should be able to analyze a situation in a matter of seconds.

Once you get the hang of this, you can start to find ways to help others AND get what you want at the same time. You'll start to see win-win solutions.

Situational-awareness is the key to getting out of the weirdovert stage. So if you now realize that you are a weirdovert, get to work on fixing this immediately. Hopefully you can dial back your attitude a bit and stop annoying people.

So far we've hopefully identified enough weirdovert behaviours to make you aware of them. Try to avoid spending too much time in Weirdovertland. It's not much fun for you or the people around you.

In summary:

1. Are you a weirdovert?
2. If you are, stop it.
3. Develop situational awareness.

Edwin's Thoughts

I had a couple of weirdovert stages. One summer I was a camp counsellor at Air Cadets and made a best friend who dressed like Kris Kross so I decided to copy him. I bought a pair of the pants that had a crotch that hung at my knees and the wild shirt. That lasted just for the summer, after which I went back to my high school. I realized the experiment was a failure and didn't try that again.

My second weirdovert stage was in university when I tried copying Dave. I was lucky to have him right beside me, helping to curb some of my enthusiasm and direct some of my efforts. Without him, I can imagine I would have been an even wilder, weirder guy.

An introvert's ability to focus helps in the learning of new skills, including the skill of extroversion. We spend so much time in our own heads, it makes it easier to watch the process happen and learn and adapt along the way. Our challenge is in working towards getting out of our own heads first, moving to situational awareness, and then to other's awareness. It takes time, energy, and practice to be able to do this on the fly. But it's really worth it.

Extroverts get a head start at being effectively outgoing because they start in kindergarten. At that time, the learning process is less onerous because everything you do as a kid is easier and has less impact. As adults trying to learn extroversion, we are more self-conscious, the pressures are greater, and the consequences are more impactful (such as needing to make a sale to put food on the table).

So use that innate ability to focus. Focus on the situation and focus on others. You will be more liked and more successful. And best of all, you will make a difference in the world. Our journeys included many people who influenced and helped us along the way. This book is about giving you another resource as you start (or continue) on your journey. The next chapters will offer you ideas and strategies for developing your ambivert muscle.

Beginning Your Journey
By Vy Tri

This chapter is a transitional one. In the earlier chapters Edwin and I shared some stories, explain our position on ambiversion, and presented a cautionary tale about weirdoverts. The following three chapters are the nuts and bolts of three essential extrovert skills that ambiverts need to adapt: small talk, talking to strangers, and the ambivert method of selling.

Here, I want to spend some time helping you establish a foundation for success on your journey. Skills can be built upon that foundation, and if ever you have doubts, you can come back to it and centre yourself. I'll divide this into two parts, mental preparation and physical appearance.

Let's start with your mental preparation. As natural introverts, we already spend a lot of time inside our own heads so this part should be easy. Or not.

Begin by examining your thoughts, beliefs, and emotions a little closer. You will need to tweak some of the wiring in your head. For some of you, it will be a major renovation. But that's ok, we all start at a different place. The important thing is we recognize that some of that wiring does need to change, and even more importantly, that we develop the courage to make that change.

Remember, I was a weirdovert for years because I refused to acknowledge that I needed to change. For me courage to change wasn't the issue. Courage to *admit* I needed to change was.

So I ask you this: Do you still know everything? Truly ask yourself if you are willing to take a step back and examine every aspect of your thinking. Do you have an air of superiority around others? Would some people think you are a bit cocky? Do you act differently in different circles?

Why? Where is that need to act that way coming from? Be honest with yourself.

If you lack confidence, are shy, and quiet around others, I also ask you: why? I know you are the way you are, but why is it so? Why is it you can be confident with some and not with others?

Did someone else really make you into this? Or did you let them influence you? If you let them influence you, that's great news because you recognized the mental choice there. You can choose a different path for yourself. That's what we're talking about here. If you can recognize that you need to change, you can choose to change.

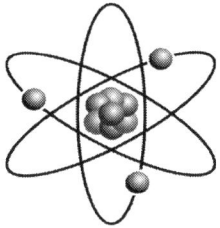

Imagine a picture of an atom. The centre of the atom is called the nucleus. That's the core and the start of the foundation we will build upon. The electrons flying around that atom are your current thoughts, beliefs, and emotions. It's the face you show the public.

Some of those electrons are definitely good thought routines and beliefs. But for now, everything is up for scrutiny. Remember, you are at this point in your life because of the culmination of your thoughts and your beliefs.

Strip those electrons away, examine your nucleus, and then slowly add electrons back. The beauty is you'll get to choose what gets added back.

Identifying your nucleus is straight forward, but not easy. People can spend their lifetime seeking this. For our purposes, I find it easier to instead think about our values.

What do you value? What makes you valuable? What value can you bring to the world? What value can you add to the lives in your immediate circle? What do you do really well? It could be multiple things, it could be one thing. There is something there that makes you, you.

Spend some time thinking about it and try to get a written definition of it. From that definition will naturally flow a goal or a purpose. To put it another way, now that you know what you value, what do you want to do with that knowledge? There's parts of you that you want to share with the world. There is some sort of impact that you'll want to make. It doesn't have to be Earth-shattering. It just has to be important to you.

Hang on to that because you'll need that goal when things get tough and you're wondering why you even want to bother with this journey.

Now, let's examine those thought processes swirling around your nucleus. Again, let's use me as an example. As I said earlier, my biggest stumbling block was that I refused to acknowledge that I needed to change. My illogical need to be right and have things my way all the time really hindered my progress.

For me, I had to take a step back, humble myself, and become a student of human psychology. Through mentorship, I realized that if I wanted to change, I had to open up my mind to suggestions from others who have accomplished the things in life I wanted.

Did this mean I had to become a mindless minion? Of course not. But it did mean I had to check my stubbornness at the door. I had to trick myself about everything by starting with: "Hypothetically, let's assume I was wrong."

Much to my amazement, I discovered that many times my reasons for believing something were unfounded. I was usually trying to justify a prior emotional decision. Ouch.

If you are like I was, just starting was my biggest challenge. Hopefully my sharing that will help some of you out.

You will not agree with everything Edwin and I want you to do in the book. That's okay. You'll find many other authorities on this subject who have some great advice, too. You'll find many gems in other personal development books.

Use the shopping cart method to learning: take what you need now. Leave the rest. You don't buy everything in the store when you go shopping, so we don't expect you do the same with this book. Just grab what you can use now. Come back later and see if anything else could be useful to you then. You're evolving as a person, so different things will strike you at different times.

Remember, no matter what advice you get, I want you to take some time and run that advice through your analytical mind. Determine if any of the new concepts have merit. Think about how you can adapt those concepts so that it will work for you. Then implement it.

Here is where the rubber meets the road. I have seen many people who look at a valid concept, but will not implement it. There is some barrier preventing them from acting. Often times they can't verbalize it. It's just an uncomfortable feeling.

99% of the time that something else is fear and/or anxiety. Anxiety is really fear of the unknown, so we're left with just fear. Maybe not the "scary dark alley" kind of fear, but fear nonetheless. There is nothing wrong with being afraid. Ask anyone who has done something brave. They will tell you that they did what they did in spite of their fear. They were afraid, but they did it anyways.

A common fear for introverts is embarrassment.

There are many types of fear. The big one for us introverts is the fear of embarrassment. Whereas extroverts can laugh off an embarrassing moment, we introverts can feel mortified. It can be debilitating. To combat this you have to realize two things:

1. No one actually cares. Other people don't walk around judging you constantly. They make a 2-second snap judgement based on your appearance, and then they go back to thinking about themselves. Everything you do from that point on doesn't matter unless it affects them directly. If you happen to embarrass yourself in front of another introvert, don't worry about it

because they will just be glad it wasn't them. They won't make any comments; they will just politely ignore you. If you happen to embarrass yourself in front of an extrovert, again, don't worry about it. They will probably make a joke, laugh with you, or else do something to draw attention away from you and onto themselves.

2. You can actually use the embarrassing moment to your advantage. Turn it into an opportunity to let others relate to you. Being vulnerable is incredibly relatable. Have you ever started talking to someone and they don't hear you, but the person standing next to them does? It's a bit embarrassing. Instead of feeling stupid, make fun of it. Maybe turn to the one who heard you and make a funny face and shrug your shoulders. Maybe pretend-wave to get the other person's attention. I guarantee you'll make someone smile. Then you can start a conversation with that person. You need to be adaptable to work with these moments. Remember, extroverts don't feel embarrassment the way we do. But with enough practice, we can appear to be just as easy-going.

Which leads us to a big key in mental preparation: planning ahead. When you go into a situation that could potentially be embarrassing, prepare ahead of time by going into "extrovert mode."

For some people, they like to think about it as pretending to be someone else. It's like putting on a stage face as if they are in a movie or a play. They go into character; they treat it like a role-play. For Edwin, he would always think "what would Dave do in this situation?"

For me, I decided to become someone else. Literally. I think they call it "method acting." But I took it to an entirely new level. There was a couple of years in school where I was not myself. My sister will attest to this.

Of the billion or so extroverts out there, I had decided to copy my best buddy, Eddy. Now to be clear, I didn't agree with everything he did, thought, or said. But I did admire his ability to make friends and be outgoing. So those traits are what I copied. I copied the mannerisms I wanted to duplicate. Back to our atom analogy for a second: while my nucleus stayed the same, I re-arranged all my electrons to look like his.

Whether you want to take it to the extreme like I did, or simply imitate an extrovert for a short period of time, it is very important that you pick someone to copy who you have direct access to and know on a personal level. You'll need to watch for their subtle gestures and discern their thought processes. This is best done while you're together. Keep your observational senses focused on the differences in how you both react to situations. Take mental notes and make adjustments to your own actions, emotions, and thought processes accordingly.

Eventually, I found that after faking the habits for so long, these habits actually became a part of me. I had managed to internalize them, and they're no longer "fake." For you sports enthusiasts, it's no different than deliberately practicing a golf swing, a throwing motion, a skating stride, etc. After a while, the mechanics just become part of how you do things. It becomes natural.

At this point, I usually get a lot of push back from introverts. They don't want to be someone else. They want to be themselves, just more outgoing. I know how you feel. I felt the same way, and here is what I found.

First, I discovered that I was just using this as an excuse to do nothing. We talked about fear earlier. When I looked deep down, I found that I was afraid of change. More than that: I was afraid that the process of changing would bring on much embarrassment. Then I realized that by committing to this journey I had already committed to dealing with embarrassment. Anytime you try something new, things can go awry. It's part of the deal. Ok then, bring it on.

Second, I also felt that I was being less than genuine. It just wasn't me. And then it hit me. I didn't like being me 100% of the time anyways. That is why I wanted to change in the first place. I had to remember that there is no rule saying I have to copy my extroverted friend right down to the last detail. There's already one Eddy and the world didn't need two (Eddy would agree). I would just copy the parts I liked. If Eddy did something that I wished I did, I went and copied that part. Sometimes I would try it and find that I didn't like it after all. Then I would delete that from my repertoire. This is a journey full of trial and error. I was building the new me with the parts I wanted. What could be more genuine than that?

Think of it as shopping for a new wardrobe at a name brand discount store like Winners, Kohls, Marshalls, etc. You start with a shopping cart, and anything that looks good or cheap or preferably both, you throw in there. Then you wheel your haul to the change rooms and try on every piece. Sometimes twice. Not everything looks as good on you as you imagined it would. Some things you picked up "just for fun" actually turn out really good when you put it on. You just never know until you try it out. In the end, you'll probably only buy 10% of the things you brought into the change room. You'll toss 90% of the things you thought would look good, and only keep the things you truly wanted. It's still you, just a better looking you.

Same thing here. You are just refining your personality, not becoming someone else.

We are just refining ourselves, not becoming someone else.

Now, I will admit that at the beginning I was acting very similar to Eddy. Eerily similar. That was because I was new to this. I jumped right in and emulated. I was still me deep down, but my exterior was closer to Eddy than the real me. When in Rome, right? I was trying things and seeing how they worked. As I observed a wider variety of extroverts in action, I gradually replaced the difference pieces with ones that suited me better. Today, Eddy and I are very different people with little in common.

At the beginning, though, I found that by adopting all of Eddy's mannerisms right away people reacted differently to me almost immediately. It's the phenomenon of the first impression. If you can manage to come across as an extrovert in your first impression, people will respond to you as if you are one. This makes the "faking it" so much easier because it gives you the green light to continue in your role. You may dial it back after your first impression, but the people you just met will always think of you as an extrovert. Edwin does this all the time as he networks for his business and charitable work. He finds it helps to know that he doesn't have to keep it up indefinitely.

Amy Cuddy, Professor at Harvard, calls it "fake it till you become it." If you haven't seen her TED talk, head over to YouTube and give it a go. It's called *Your body language shapes who you are*.

You've probably heard that non-verbal communication (physical appearance, facial expression, and body language) governs how other people think and feel about us. Professor Cuddy takes this one step further and shows us that these non-verbals also influence how we think and feel about *ourselves*. By simply tweaking our body language we can change our mental state for a short time. When you force yourself to smile, you start to feel happy. When you pretend to be powerful, you actually feel powerful.

The body can control the mind. By changing your physical appearance and body language, you can change who you are. By adopting good extroverted traits you can become more extroverted. You really can fake it, or as I prefer to think of it: "practice it" until you become it.

This leads us into the second major area you need to prepare: your physical outward appearance. As introverts, we often wish we were invisible, and so we try to hide within our dress code. Many true introverts dress poorly. Colours clash, clothes are too baggy, hair is not well maintained, and (for men?) there is lots of unkempt facial hair. If you wear glasses, chances are they are big and obscure much of your face. We justify it with some variation of "I want to be comfortable." Unfortunately, your comfort does not make you an interesting target for conversation or a leadership role.

The way you dress matters.

On the other end of the spectrum, some introverts dress outrageously in order to get attention. Unfortunately, it has the opposite effect. People will only stare at you and do their best to avoid you. Remember, that's weirdovert behaviour. Resist it at all costs.

Having said that, it's okay to wear something that is interesting, but classy. It's certainly acceptable to add some flair that is remarkable. The key is it has to be in good taste. It's a fine line. Don't worry if you don't have a clue right now, you'll realize the difference as you start to focus on it during your journey.

In case you didn't get it: lose the funny t-shirt and don't wear a Dr. Seuss hat in public. But if you have a necklace, wrist band, or a pin that could be a conversation starter, go ahead and show it off.

People generally respond better when you look sharp and confident. So shave even if you don't think you need to (this also goes for women). Get your hair cut. If you prefer to wear your hair long, then get an actual hair style. Remember, you have less than 2-seconds to make a first impression.

If you are like most introverts, you will need a complete revamp of your wardrobe. Figure out your actual clothes size and get clothes that fit. If you don't know, then go to the store and start trying on outfits. Here's a tip: sales people will help you. It's their job to sell you things that look good on you. From now on, you don't buy any clothing that you haven't tried on first. Even a belt. This goes double for when you see something in your size and you "just know" it will fit. Every brand has a different take on size. Plus you may have gained or lost weight since you last purchased something in your "normal size."

If you don't have the budget, go to discount stores like I mentioned earlier. However, be aware that these places don't have sales staff to help. In that event, bring a fashion-conscious friend. Task them with the job of making you look good regardless of your personal preferences and protestations. As is obvious to them, you have no eye for proper dress. The only reason you shouldn't buy something they suggest is budget. After you get better at dressing, then (and only then) should you make your own fashion decisions. Everything being equal, my suggestion is to start at the nice stores with sales people who know what they are doing.

I can't emphasize enough how important this step is. It's like being an actor and not having the right costume for the part. Or playing a sport and not having the right gear. You're not as effective as you can be. You have to get your dress right.

If you need more convincing, think of it this way: Instead of hiding in your bad clothes and looking weird, hide in your nice clothes. You'll look good doing it, and if you feel anti-social that day, then don't talk to anyone. However, by dressing nice, you'll always have the option in case your mood changes.

That's it... except just like Steve Job's famous line, there's one more thing! It's quite important so I wanted to emphasize it. Here it is: Always say "yes" when some asks if you want to do something.

I know, I know. This can be dangerous, but it will speed up your journey. You will get the most bang for your buck right here. When someone asks you to go with them, it's because they want company. They value your camaraderie. By always saying "yes" you automatically become cool in their eyes. Maybe they're going to something that makes them a bit nervous. Maybe they're trying to be nice to you. Maybe they're just lonely. It doesn't matter the reason. But if you agree to go with them, you will build a deeper connection. Right there. That's what we crave as introverts: deeper connections.

As a side benefit, these outings are the perfect opportunity to practice your extrovert skills. If you're out in public, you can do all the things we write about in the next three chapters: small talk, talking to strangers, and sales. All of these activities need to be done with other people. Since you're already with someone, that makes things easier.

Talking to strangers while you're in the company of another person actually makes it two-times easier. The embarrassment factor is halved because you're both lumped together. If one of you talks to a stranger, it's the equivalent of both of you doing it. If you get the cold shoulder, then you can fall back to talking to your friend. If your friend engages first, that's a bonus. Don't forget to take notes on what they did.

Say yes more often.

When you're out and about with someone you have strength in numbers and can take more chances. Your friend will bail you out. This works even if you're both introverts. Even if it's just lunch with a co-worker. Practice your small talk then.

If you end up in a group, try to persuade them about something. As Edwin will show you, persuasion is a form of sales. As author Daniel Pink says, *To sell is human*.

So always go out. Even when you don't feel like it. I should say, especially when you don't feel like it. You may just need to recharge, or you may just be lazy. But you can do that when your friends don't need you. They're asking for a reason. So go.

Personally, I always said "no" because I was afraid of the social situation. I let my fear hold me back. Sometimes it was something as dumb as fear of driving at night, or fear of not knowing the route. But almost every time I went when I didn't feel like it, I always felt better afterwards.

In the end, you never know what will happen. Possible adventure and hijinks await.

The stories I've shared with you are meant to give you confidence. Preparation increases confidence. Having company multiplies confidence. That's why people are brave in groups. We'll delve more into confidence in the next chapter.

For now, suffice to say confidence will suppress fear. Less fear means you'll be able to step out of your comfort zone and begin trying extroverted things. I said "less fear," not "no fear." You only have to suppress fear just long enough to allow action.

To summarize:

1. Be coachable & take suggestions.
2. Combat fear by "going into character."
3. Copy the behaviours you like; leave the rest.
4. Dress sharp.
5. Always say "yes" to going out.

Edwin's Thoughts

So why are you reading this book? Your ambivert journey needs motivation. There are no shortcuts to anyplace worth going, and this is a very worthwhile endeavour. If you can keep your ultimate goal up in front of you, it's easier to go through the steps.

Our motivations revolved around being successful, putting food on our families' tables, and making a difference in the world. These are easier to do when you are an ambivert because you will be involved in more things.

While going through your journey, you have to be true to certain parts of yourself. If you are introvert, you can't become an extrovert 100% of the time. Learn what parts of yourself you need to keep. For most of us, it's the need to spend some time at rest, alone, or in a less stimulated place. Then you will have the energy to put in the effort for those times when you are outside of your normal state.

I love Vy Tri's emphasis on first impressions. They are not just important, but critical. It's way easier to do the first 10 seconds of an interaction right than have to change that first impression. So before meeting someone for the first time, take a second to remind yourself of what you are trying to accomplish. If it's work related, what type of person are you trying to be? If it's at a party, don't start off as shy – you can do that later. If it's in a classroom, make your first interaction with the professor a good one – not whining about a certain assignment.

In her book, *Bossypants*, Tina Fey talks about one of the key tenets to improvisation is also a key to life. The main rule of improv is to say "yes and" instead of "no but." When doing a scene with someone, and they make a suggestion, if you say "no but" you have broken the rhythm and it's harder for the other person to continue. They have to put in more effort and thought to keep the conversation and the skit flowing.

Saying "yes and" signifies that you are a team player and that others can count on you. It's easier to be around a person who goes with the flow instead of someone who is a blocker. If you block, people stop engaging with you because it takes more effort to be around you.

By saying "yes" to life, you will automatically be more extroverted. And as a side benefit, saying "yes" usually results in more happiness.

One of the biggest things I've learned in life, and continue to learn, is that other people are rarely thinking about you. We all tend to think the world revolves around "me." But it doesn't. Out of sight, out of mind in most cases so stop stressing about the screw ups.

A key part to Ambiversion is our ability to have meaningful and impactful conversations. The next chapter will give you some great tools and techniques to make it easier for you to become a great conversationalist.

Small Talk

By Vy Tri

"So you weren't born with that essential ingredient of charm, the gift of gab. So what? Few are.... Conversation is an acquired skill. If you have the determination and the proper information, just like any other skill, it can be learned."

- Keith Ferrazzi – *Never Eat Alone: And Other Secrets to Success, One Relationship at a Time*

According to Keith Ferrazzi, one of the best networkers and most connected people in the world, only a few of us were born with the gift of the gab. The rest of us have to learn it.

For many introverts, this comes as a surprise. A divine revelation even. From the outside looking in, small talk can appear as a special talent. Some people have it, some don't. While that may have some truth to it, it should not be a limiting factor for you. Just like any other skill, it can be learned with enough study and focused practice.

Only a few of us were born with the gift of the gab. The rest of us have to learn it.

When studying small talk, pay attention to not only the questions asked, but also the intonations and the pace of the conversation. Often when I listen to people who are good at small talk, I am mesmerized on how skilled they are at asking questions and connecting. I have to catch myself at those times and force myself to pay attention to why it is working.

I love structure, so I find it quite helpful to try and find some structure in the conversation. It may be quite loose if friends are meeting or quite formal if it's a business lunch. Either way, try to find the method in the madness.

At the beginning, you may have to sit down at a desk and take some notes with pad and pencil. Make notes about the extroverts in your life and how they do it. You studied them in the last chapter, but now drill down to the specifics of how they conduct a conversation. Practice the questions they ask to see how they sound coming from your mouth. It might be a bit odd, so tweak it to suit your style. There's nothing wrong with talking to yourself (as long as you do it in private).

Before you are fully ready, and while you are still uncomfortable, you should conduct a few practice sessions with people in the real world. Why then? Because it's important to test your assumptions before you become married to them. Just like we talked about in the previous chapter, you should be constantly testing and refining.

The refining part is much more difficult than the testing part. To use a sports analogy, refining means conducting a full debrief and reviewing the game footage. Reflect privately about the process and results of your efforts. If possible, bring in a friend or a coach and ask for their feedback.

I spent years as a weirdovert because I never did this part. Once I started to reflect and analyze the results of my interactions, I was finally able to see where I was going wrong. I was finally able to come to terms with myself.

Studying, testing, practicing, and refining is a concept that works in all disciplines and across all cultures. It's a universal concept of improvement. Leaders use it to build entire industries. This idea can be taken to the micro-scale and used to improve your own abilities in small talk.

It's true. Being naturally witty and having things to say can be adequately simulated with enough study, practice, and preparation. It takes the same skill and determination as it does to learn a sport, acquire job skills, or raise a family.

The most common thing we hear about elite athletes is that they practice more than anyone else. They're obsessed with their sport. How about CEO's? Same thing. Always at the office first, and last to leave. They're constantly working. That's how they got there. Movie, music, and comedic stars all have one thing in common: they work extremely hard at their craft. They put in more behind the scenes hours than some people do at work actually working. From the outside looking in, it appears as if they are naturals. All you see is fruits of that labour.

If you've ever been in a long-term relationship you understand that you constantly have to work at building that relationship. If you've raised a family, you understand that you continually have to teach your kids. What the outside world sees is the finished product not the mess you left at home.

Everything that matters in life requires hard work.

Everything that matters in life requires hard work. In my opinion, your transformation from introvert to ambivert is one of the most important things you'll ever do.

Before we get into the structure of a small talk conversation, let's talk about why we do it in the first place. What is the point of small talk?

You probably have some extremely introverted friends who see no point in it, and think it's a stupid waste of time.

For them, they are right. For their circumstance and for what they want out of life, they do not need small talk.

But since you're reading this book, you want something different. The world is full of people and in order to get ahead, you need to navigate people effectively.

Small talk gives you the ability to find ways to connect with those people and relate to them. People help others whom they like and with whom they can find a personal bond.

Picture your most extroverted friends. Not other ambiverts, but true extroverts. One of the first things you'll notice about them is their ability to turn off the filter between their brain and their mouth. Now, this filter does come on, depending on the situation, but its default position is "off." As an introvert whose thoughts and opinions are treasured and extremely private, this can be quite a shock.

I remember one of the first times I noticed that my best buddy, Eddy the extrovert, would admit his mistake out loud. "Oh, I didn't know Austria and Australia are different countries! Doh!"

My first thought was "Why on Earth would you admit that you were wrong?" I would have been so embarrassed. But while Eddy admitted to it and laughed it off, I would have let it eat away at me, thinking, "oh crap, don't let anyone find out that I'm a geographic luddite."

Surprisingly, the reaction to Eddy's comment was, "ha ha, you're a bit of a dummy sometimes. Oh well, move on."

Was that so bad? No, not at all. Did any harm come to his reputation? Nope. In fact, over time, I noticed that doing these things actually helped people relate to Eddy better. It helped him get more friends. It made him likeable.

Let's take a closer look at this phenomenon.

People prefer to be around others with whom they can relate. Imagine if you will, a giant invisible suitcase that we carry around everywhere we go. This suitcase contains our likes, dislikes, insecurities, experiences, thoughts, and passions. As we travel through life, we tend to find others with the same kind of baggage and we make a connection. We develop camaraderie.

Introverts, by nature, guard their suitcases like Fort Knox. We're talking not only those silly little luggage locks (where all the keys in the world are the same) but also padlocks, deadbolts, bicycle chains, and an armed guard under an invisibility cloak.

Extroverts, meanwhile, have a duffel bag emblazoned with stickers from everywhere they've been. The zipper is broken and their underwear is hanging out. And they're oblivious to all of this. Occasionally something falls out, but they shrug it off, knowing that they'll replace it down the road if it is important.

Being a typical extrovert, Eddy was sharing everything he thought. He was giving us insight into the contents of his duffel bag. Anyone looking in could see potential connections and similarities with their own luggage contents. To continue the metaphor, if you had some of the same carry-on items, you would think to yourself, "this guy is pretty cool." The more glimpses you get, the deeper the bond can become.

So paradoxically, by being wrong and talking about it, Eddy was doing the right thing. People connect with honesty. They see you're real, not smooth. By showing his flaws and turning them into humorous moments, he was making it easier for others to relate. Extroverts are constantly throwing out all these opportunities for potential connections as they meander through life. Is it any wonder they pickup so many friends along the way?

The lesson here isn't to have no filter at all. (Remember, I said extroverts are selective with it.) It's that you need to guard your thoughts *less* closely. Loosen up and take yourself *less* seriously. When you don't know something, chances are there are other people in the room who don't know either. You just have to be brave enough to admit it.

We have the same fears as you.

I have that same fear you have. My mind tells me that the room will turn towards me and laugh and point. This has maybe happened to me once or twice in all my years. And in both instances, people thought I was making a joke.

Every other time, the reaction was one of support because one or two other people didn't know either. Sometimes even half the room chimed in. Unbeknownst to me at the time, these actions actually helped others relate to me.

Because people heard from me (even if it was just me stating my ignorance) they felt like they could talk to me. By saying something, anything, I was in essence giving others a look into my suitcase.

Relatability is a key tenant in leadership. If you are in such a position, or aspire to be, then it is vital that you are relatable to as many stakeholders as possible. You have to share enough of yourself so that others can find some connection points.

I had a boss who would only focus on the issues at hand. When we had our "coaching sessions" he would ask me about my thoughts and my life, but he never shared anything from his. So I always felt like there was a bit of a wall there. We didn't need to be best friends (and probably shouldn't be given our positions) but it would've helped me understand where he was coming from on some issues.

The lesson here is to share enough to build connections. Small talk leads to relatability, which builds relationships. This is why it's so important to develop good small talk. Small talk occurs during those breaks inside a serious conversation.

With that as a foundation, let's get into the conversation itself. As we talked about earlier, there is a certain structure to small talk. It may be hard to find as there is a lot going on in any given conversation.

The first part is the initial pleasantries. If you are meeting a long-time friend, it's probably more like a welcome. If you're meeting on business, it's probably thanking them for their time and a comment about the weather.

From there, immediately move into the introductions. If you have others with you, be sure to introduce them. This is the perfect time to engage in a bit of small talk. After that, summarize why you are meeting and thank them for meeting you. This goes for both personal and business settings. It gives the conversation a place to start.

From there, the conversation will have a life of its own. It will be a back and forth where you'll explore the various topics of the meeting. Questions will be asked, stories will be shared, and commonality will be found. In a personal setting, there may not be a formal agenda. So follow the conversation where it may take you.

However, in a business setting, there is always a specific goal. Here, you'll want to follow this loose structure:

- Small talk.
- Direct the conversation to a key topic with a question.
- Acknowledge and summarize the answer.
- Respond with your points.
- Direct the conversation back to relevant small talk with a question.

Repeat this structure until the key topics are addressed, or until it's time to conclude. I recommend you conclude with a follow-up. It could be booking another meeting, or it could be a promise to do something. More on this later.

Did you notice that we directed the conversation with questions? Good question asking is vital to having a good conversation.

There are two keys to good question asking. The first, which we covered in earlier chapters is you must have a genuine interest in others. The second is you have to adopt a student mentality again. Seek to learn about others. Find out how they got to their position in life, why they think the way they do, and what else they've seen in the world. Those are all amazing topics. Be curious and ask questions to find out more.

Seek to learn about others.

There is a real art form to good question-asking. You must practice this a lot. Take notes when someone asks you a good question. Pay attention to what the good question-askers around you do.

If you're anything like me, you'll probably ask some stupid questions at first. "Oh you have a dog. What kind of dog is it? Is that a big dog? What colour is your dog? What does your dog like to eat?"

After awhile you'll refine your questioning skills. "Excuse my ignorance, but I'm not familiar with that type of dog. Could you describe him?" Don't play 20 questions. Make it a two-way interaction. Follow the conversation by asking follow-up questions that are on-topic. Ask open-ended questions where possible. That is, ask questions that can't be answered by a "yes" or "no." Let the other person talk and see where they take the conversation.

Pauses and silences will come up. Even though you are trying to find something relatable to say or a question to ask, sometimes, there's just nothing. That's okay.

Here's a trick I learned to buy some time. It's called "interesting…" After someone says something and looks at you for your turn to speak, you respond with an interested-sounding "interesting…." Say it in such a way where it allows the other person to continue talking.

"I love my cat, but she drives me nuts."

"Really? That's Interesting…"

"Yeah, so yesterday she was just ignoring me. I have no idea what I did to make her mad."

"Huh. Interesting…"

"I know, right? So blah blah blah"

What's great about "interesting…" is it's non-committal. By saying it, you aren't agreeing with what the other person is saying. You are not putting them down or debasing their ideas. It's completely non-judgemental, and you aren't taking any sides. You're completely on the fence here.

The example above is quite silly. However, the point is it can be used as a stall tactic to give you a second to formulate a response or ask another question. It keeps the conversation going and avoids those awkward silences.

This works in a business setting as well. I've used it as a segue to direct the conversation.

"Interesting… Why do you feel that way?"

"It's interesting you should say that, we've found that…"

You never want to judge, as you may lose the other person before you have a chance to bring up your points. "Interesting…" acknowledges their thoughts and allows them to continue or clarify if necessary. You can then segue to your thoughts and direct the conversation.

There is a psychology to it as well. We all love talking about ourselves. Introverts, extroverts, ambiverts, weirdoverts, it doesn't matter. It's a human thing. And the more we talk, the more we think the conversation went well. Amazingly enough, when we get into a groove and talk a lot, we think the OTHER person is a good conversationalist.

This makes question-asking an introvert's best friend. You avoid talking about yourself, AND the other person thinks you're great company. But don't go to the extreme. Remember to insert some commentary and relatability points. Keep it short though and keep the conversation flowing. It's like verbal tennis: keep putting the ball back in their court.

This works in a group of people as well. For example, at a dinner party where there is some unfamiliarity, you can go around the table with questions, and help the other guests find commonalities with each other. You don't actually have to say anything about yourself, and everyone will think of you as the life of the party.

People who make the best conversationalists genuinely like and enjoy the company of others. Remember that everyone you meet is your superior in one way or another. Try to find their unique specialty.

This means you can still have great conversations with people who annoy you. Just remember that they are simply doing the best they can with what they have. Try to see the world from their point of view. Focus on their good points. Reach if you have to. You only need to keep it up for the short time you are required to be in their company.

The best conversationalists genuinely like and enjoy the company of others.

Fundamental to feeling comfortable in front of others and being able to ask good questions is personal self-confidence. You need that inner belief in yourself. You have to know that you are an awesome person, and you have a lot to offer the world. Know that you can do anything when you put your mind to it. You are a rock, and nothing that happens today can change that.

When you have confidence in yourself, you don't have to act like a peacock. Peacocks make a spectacle of showing off their plumage to impress other people. Peacock Syndrome is real and it's annoying. Cockiness is a symptom of Peacock Syndrome. Weirdoverts have a bad case of this illness.

Confident people see no need and have no desire to show off to others. Having confidence means you can take the focus off yourself and put it on other people. It allows you to put your insecurities aside and concentrate on what others have to offer.

To illustrate, let's say you have a lack of confidence. As soon as you were put in a situation where you need to make small talk, you would freeze up. Your mind would blank out. You would all of a sudden become self-conscious. In your head, you scream at yourself: "say somethiiiiiing!" In short, what is happening is you are focused on yourself. You are trying to think of something to say about yourself that might be interesting to the other person. This is not conducive to small talk.

The other person doesn't care so much about your personal insecurities. They care about their own insecurities. They carry around their own baggage, and they want to talk about it. Your job in a conversation is to bring that out of the other person, not talk about your own stuff. Yes, you have to share things about yourself to be relatable, but the difference is the intent. Are you sharing to relate or are you sharing to brag?

If you lack self-confidence, is hard to focus on others. I've been there and lived it. I understand that you feel like you have to validate yourself to everyone you meet. Deep down, you're trying to justify your own existence and show people your worth. I get it. It's something I've had to work through, and if you're like me, you'll have to work through it as well.

Personally, I had to read a lot of books that addressed my self-confidence issues. When I learned about the thoughts of successful people, and how they lined up with my own views, it validated me. Discovering that I have the same views as some of the most successful people in the world gave me confidence.

When you are confident in yourself, you feel liberated. All your energy can and does become focused on the environment around you.

Take golf for instance. A golfer who lacks confidence will have a million thoughts go through his head as he addresses the ball: relax your shoulders, hands forward, widen your stance, practice the back swing, nice and smooth, don't screw this up, you've been slicing everything today so adjust your hips, etc. It just goes on and on. There's too much to think about. How could you possibly execute a good stroke when your mind is bombarding you with all those messages?

Compare that to the confident golfer. Before he addresses the ball, he has a look around. He takes into consideration how the course is laid out, the condition of the grass, the effect of the wind, what kind of spin he needs to put on the ball, etc. And when he addresses the ball, all he's looking for is the feel. As soon as it feels right, he swings. There is no second guessing. He's just relying on the muscle memory from hours of practice. He stops thinking about all the little things and just does the one important thing: hitting the ball.

Notice how the confident golfer focused his energies outward, while in the first example, the nervous golfer is focused inward. Same thing with small talk.

No one starts with 100% self-confidence. It comes with time. You will develop the "muscle memory." Just keep practicing and pulling yourself out of your comfort zone.

Self-confidence starts with your self-talk.

To gain confidence, you really have to watch your own self-talk. Self-talk is what you say to yourself. As introverts, we tend to get caught up in all our mistakes and short comings. We dwell on them and chastise ourselves for them. This doesn't help our confidence. Instead, you need to speak positively to yourself. Make personal affirmations, also known as self-worth statements. Use powerful words that move you. Yes, it's very cheesy, but your subconscious doesn't know that. Cheese works, that's why it's in so many movies and books. Control your self-talk, and you will control your world. You will find this theme in every success book.

One way to quickly gain confidence is preparation. When I first started a new job, I didn't have confidence because I wasn't familiar with how things worked. After a couple of months, my interactions were much different. I was going after the sale.

Preparation leads to confidence. This is also true with small talk. When it's your turn to talk and you need to share something relatable, that part needs to be prepared.

The topic could be a commentary on a current world event, a current industry trend, or simply what's new in pop culture. It could be a perfect opportunity to share a past experience or a short story.

I can confidently tell you that this will not be a problem for you. Why? Because you are an introvert and introverts prepare like no one else on earth.

If you are one of those people who find that they have a hard time coming up with things to talk about, all you have to do is put some effort into preparation.

Before you leave the house, find some things to talk about. Perhaps you ran across something on a social media site, the television, or even the radio. It doesn't have to be earth shattering, just something of interest to you. Possible ideas could be:

1. Trending pop culture topic. Maybe it's time for the Grammy's or the Oscar's. Maybe some famous person did something outrageous. Have a look at the top trending hash-tags on Twitter.
2. Current news items. Stay away from deaths, tragedies, politics, and finances. Instead, talk about new inventions, medical breakthroughs, real

estate, or some other neutral but interesting topics. Remember, it's small talk so keep it light.
3. New books, TV shows, or movies. "Have you seen such and such," or "I can't wait for this or that," are great little topics.
4. Something funny/interesting/embarrassing that you, your kids, or other family members did recently. Any epic fails or great accomplishments?
5. Recent events in sports. Is there a controversy? Did one team upset another?
6. Recent things you've purchased. What is the best bargain that you found recently? Any new stores worth mentioning?
7. New activities. Did you discover a new sport or recreational activity? Have a new cause that you're passionate about?

Having about three of these things in the back of your mind will put you at ease when you visit with someone. You can relax and enjoy the conversation because you know when it's your turn, you will have at least three interesting things to talk about.

These same ideas also work in a business context. There's always a bit of small talk before or after a meeting. That's the perfect time to engage with whoever is in the room. It shows you're not a corporate stiff, and allows others to relate to you just a little bit more.

I had a tough time with this initially because I was all business. After observing some of my colleagues, it became clear that business is about relationships, and relationships start with small talk.

Always stay on top of your industry trends. There are often one or two newsletters everyone subscribes to, which makes it an easy place to find topics for a bit of small talk.

These topics are great for short visits. But if you're having a meal together, you will need something more substantial to keep the conversation going after you've blown through these ideas.

Careful preparation makes things a lot easier.

Again, preparation comes into play. You know that friend who keeps telling the same jokes, stories, and anecdotes over and over again? And it's only funny to people who haven't heard it before? Yeah. Find yourself a few of those to use. They come in handy in small talk. Don't just wing it, though, prepare it.

Take note of how they tell stories. Notice your friend's facial expressions? Their body language? Any arms flailing around? How about the cadence of their speech? How do they set you up for the punch line? Study the mannerisms and copy it. Remember, you're not a clone, but until you develop your own style, try to copy things that work.

My advice is to come up with three stories you can use in different circumstances. These can be topics you bring up "spontaneously." Alternatively, they can provide you with material to use in order to contribute meaningfully to a conversation. Here are some suggestions for stories:

1. Something funny from work. Everyone talks about work. Most of it surrounds how mentally deficient their co-workers or bosses are. Have one or two funny anecdotes to tell. Everyone can relate to these stories and you'll be able to start an entirely new conversation thread with a good story. Make it a story though; don't whine and complain. Your audience might think you could be bad mouthing them behind their backs. So keep it light.
2. Funny story about your kids or spouse. Family is one of those super easy to relate to topics. Many people have kids and spouses who do really silly things. A good story here can lead to a good 30-minute conversation.
3. Latest vacation. People love to live vicariously through others. If you've been somewhere exotic, talk about it. Colour-in the details and make it life-like. Exaggerate a bit; they'll never know. You can follow-up by finding out if the other person has been there or if they want to go. The vacation conversation can go in so many good directions. What are your future vacation plans? What have you always wanted to do?
4. A great personal accomplishment. What could be better than a story of human triumph? Have you won any trophies? Did you climb to the top of something? Maybe you just completed your first 10 KM run. Recently lost a bunch of weight or kept

it off for a long time? Committed to doing something and saw it through? It doesn't have to be a recent story. It just has to be an interesting one. Super Bowl champions tell the same story over and over again. Not many people have won one, so it's an interesting topic.

5. Sports, hobbies, pastimes, and other commitments. How do you spend your free time? Are you really good at knitting ugly Christmas sweaters? Do you do volunteer work? Maybe tell an interesting story about how you got started in your extracurricular activities.

6. Most embarrassing moment. This is a toughie. You have to have supreme confidence in order to share this one. You will be making fun of yourself. Make sure to continue the story after the embarrassing moment so that you have some sort of redemption. Or at least a scape-goat.

Whatever you chose, make it a story. Don't just talk about a topic: entertain and perform. Plan it and create some drama. Modulate your voice and use body language. Make sure you practice it repeatedly and out loud. Even if your spouse rolls their eyes. I promise you that if you know what you're going to say, and have practiced it enough times, you'll be able to perform it like a superstar. With a few canned stories in your arsenal, you will approach any situation with confidence.

The two lists above might seem a bit much to ask. After all, who can memorize seven short stories and six long stories?

That's actually not the point. I don't expect you to have all of that prepared on day one. You already have some stories and the rest you'll build up over time.

Moreover, you're a work in progress and so are your stories. Start with two or three interesting short topics and at least one dinner story. That's four things you can talk about.

In time, you will find that after using your four starting topics, they will become second nature to you. Your initial four topics will be on autopilot thus freeing up your concentration capacity. This allows you to prepare and practice new stories. You'll add new things, and as you use them, they too, will be committed to memory.

We are all a work in progress.

After a while you'll find that you have plenty of things to talk about and you have some really good stories to share. In fact, if you don't watch it, you might find yourself starting to dominate conversations. You will have become a natural.

Through all this, you must keep in mind that small talk needs to remain positive. Sure you may have negative things to say about a topic, but keep it from being a "bitch-fest." Don't complain and whine. Negative energy like that will make people want to be around you less and less. Eric Barker (bakadesuyo.com) says, "Look at it like the Hippocratic Oath of conversations: *Do no harm*."

Like all good things, the conversation must end at some point. But don't let it just fade away. If it's a relationship you value and would like to build on, I believe you should try to book a follow-up. In a business setting, it's where you set a plan of action for your next contact. In a personal context, it's getting an idea of when you'll get together again, normally an upcoming birthday, or social gathering. Or maybe there is no upcoming event, and you'll promise to get a hold of each other at a later date. If you had a great connection, it's natural to want to continue it.

"It was great chatting with you guys today. When will we be seeing you again?"

"It was nice to meet you. What's the best way for us to connect?"

We'll meet my friend Ryan in the next chapter, but one thing he taught me was how nice this follow up feels. I've always felt a bit empty when saying bye to people because the interaction just ends. Ryan showed me the difference when you conclude with a follow up. The promise of a future interaction gives you a nice warm fuzzy feeling.

To summarize:

1. Conversation is an acquired skill, so work at it.
2. Share enough of yourself to build a connection. It's like verbal tennis.
3. Use "interesting…" to keep the conversation going or to stall while you think of a question.
4. Prepare.

5. Start with a few topics, expand your repertoire over time.
6. Confidence comes from practice, so practice a lot.
7. Do no harm.
8. Conclude with a follow up.

Edwin's Thoughts

Vy Tri is great at small talk. He's personable, engaging, always keeps the conversation flowing, and makes everyone feel comfortable. I didn't know that he had to work so hard at it because he seems like a natural.

The ability to reflect is a key to learning and implementing new ideas. Not in a "poor me, I shouldn't have said that" way but in a way that is constructive. What did I do right? What went wrong? What story am I never going to repeat? What story can I borrow from another person? What did the rest of the group find most interesting?

Without taking time to reflect on your attempts at small talk, you won't improve. Replay conversations in your head to see what worked and how to refine them.

Vy Tri's comments around confidence are dear to my heart. As my story showed, I grew up confident. My Mom hammered it into me that I'm good enough and smart enough. Unfortunately, I didn't temper that confidence and it turned into cockiness.

People enjoy confident people – it makes them feel secure. Confidence is about inner peace and isn't about comparing yourself to the people around you. Other people don't feel less than you when you have confidence. Cockiness on the other hand, is all relative. Cockiness isn't about "I'm good," instead, it's about "I'm better than you." It makes others feel like they are less than you. For the majority of my life, I was cocky. It seems to work, but in the end, it's fleeting. The negative feelings it generates in others will more than offset anything positive.

Lastly, I really like the emphasis on the need to get others to talk about themselves. It's easier on you, and it makes them feel good. One important idea that I've been thinking about a lot is the idea of contempt. When doing small talk, you will inevitably find people that you think are annoying and have little to add to your life. You will think that you are smarter than them and begin to feel bored listening to them.

But even those people have a story. If you think that you are better than them, they will sense it, and your conversation and relationship will go poorly. Everyone is doing the best with what they have. Their life experiences have crafted their story, and it's interesting. Maybe they don't know as much as you do about a certain topic, but they will know something you don't.

Talking to Strangers
By Vy Tri

If we consider small talk as the regular season in sports, then talking to strangers is like the playoffs. The intensity ratchets up quite significantly and there's a lot more on the line.

Talking to strangers is probably one of the most difficult and intense things for an introvert to do. It's unnatural and extremely nerve wracking. It's so far outside of your comfort zone that you can see Pluto from there. However, and you will have to trust me on this one, you will find it to be one of the most rewarding areas you can master.

Strangers can satisfy your need to learn about diverse new things. The people you don't know do all sorts of interesting things; they've been to, or are from, remote parts of the world; they have different cultural influences; they talk differently. Their point of view on a problem or situation is extremely refreshing. For an introvert, this injection of new knowledge and fresh perspective is like Red Bull: it gives you wings.

The bottom line is strangers can open doors in your mind you never knew where there.

To overcome your fear of strangers, you have to realize that strangers are regular people. They're just new to you. They're not aliens. (Well, maybe some are.) "Strangers" doesn't always mean someone at the bar. It could be someone you talk to at Starbucks or maybe someone in your yoga class. Any person you don't know qualifies.

Talking to strangers is both an art and a science.

Talking to strangers is both art and science. You can't just wing it. Extroverts do it naturally, introverts don't do it, weirdoverts scare people off, and ambiverts plan it. You need to think about the situation, and you need to use every shred of human psychology you possess. I will illustrate with the following fictitious scenario. (Seriously, it's not me in this one.)

You're at the mall sitting at a bench waiting for your wife to come out of a store. A stranger sits down next to you and asks if you'd like a cookie and holds out a Tupperware container. What's your first reaction? If you're like most people, you'd probably decline, get up quickly, and walk away. Holy crap, that guy was a weirdo!

That was how NOT to do it in a nut shell.

Now picture the same scenario, but with a twist. You're still waiting for your wife, but this time the stranger sits down and makes a comment such as: "My wife wanted me to go to the underwear store with her, so I wished her luck and came out here instead."

You're more likely to have a bit of a chuckle and make a comment yourself. Then the stranger smiles and introduces himself. "Hi, I'm Mark." Naturally you guys continue the conversation by talking about women and shopping, how men view the event, and perhaps the differences between men and women.

Then Mark says, "Oh, by the way, my wife made some cookies to bribe me to come with her. Would you like one?" He offers you the container. Chances are pretty good that you'll take a cookie.

What happened? In both circumstances you were offered a cookie by a stranger, but in the second scenario you were much more likely to take the cookie. Why?

Let's break down this little event:

1. Mark broke the ice with a funny comment. It was something you could build on. Mark invited you into a low-risk conversation.

2. He smiled and introduced himself. Once you knew his name, he was no longer a stranger.
3. This allowed you to have a short nothing conversation and develop some rapport.
4. You had some fun which gave you the conclusion that Mark wasn't a serial killer.
5. All the warning signs in your head turned off and you felt safe taking the cookie.

Pretty cool, eh? Notice how Mark wasn't pushy with the cookie? He built a connection first by finding some common ground. Maybe if he didn't like you, he wouldn't offer the cookie. The cookie wasn't the point of the encounter. It developed as a result of what happened in the encounter. Now, I'm not advocating that you walk around with cookies. This is merely an analogy for many circumstances where you might need to talk to strangers.

- Networking event, cookie = business card or future appointment.
- School/sports, cookie = contact information.
- Party, cookie = agreement to meet up later.
- Sales, cookie = sale or follow-up appointment.

As you can see, there are lots of situations where you'll want to reach out and talk to new people. It's a skill where you'll really need to stretch your comfort zone in order to develop.

Just like in the earlier chapters, you need to start with the end in mind. Visualize someone you know who is good at talking to strangers. In a situation like this, it is always better to have an actual person to imitate rather than a made-up vision of what you think that person is like. There are so many nuances to this skill that you can't learn simply by thinking about it.

I am lucky to have a friend who is very good at this. I will call him Ryan. Ryan loves talking to strangers. It's like he has no fear. No, that's not quite right; it's more like he's oblivious to fear. "Oh, you're not supposed to just talk to random people? Oh... why not? Too late, I just did."

Ryan isn't a weirdo. In fact, he's the most laid-back person you'll meet. He's got a disarming, aw-shucks demeanour about him. You will always find Ryan in jeans, a t-shirt, a ball cap, and always holding a travel mug. He's not threatening, doesn't come across as too cool, and generally looks approachable and helpful.

Ryan selectively turns off the filter between his brain and his mouth, depending on the situation. He'll make any number of comments while in close proximity to another human being. It could be in a check-out line, in a locker room, at a coffee shop, or in a grocery aisle. It doesn't matter.

These comments, much like our Mark example above, are typically funny, nothing comments that give the other person ample opportunity to respond in kind. Some people don't respond, and if that's the case, he moves on. Like water off a duck's back.

If they do respond, he sticks around and continues to engage for as long as the conversation has legs. After three to five exchanges, he'll introduce himself and give a little background to why he's there. "Hi, I'm Ryan and I'm just out Christmas shopping. How about you? Got your shopping done?" It's easy, low-key stuff.

By observing people who are comfortable talking to strangers, you really get a sense of what works and what doesn't. It saves you a lot of trial and error. By paying attention, you'll avoid a lot of embarrassment. But you still have to practice and see what works for you.

To be effective, it is vital that you look approachable. This encompasses everything about your outward appearance from your dress to your demeanour. Fortunately, this is the easiest area to work on. All you need is a mirror.

Look approachable.

We covered dress earlier so I won't get into too much detail here. Remember that you have to look at yourself from the other person's point of view. If you were approached by someone who looks like you, how would you react? Would you respond better to someone asking you a question wearing an undershirt, swim shorts, and flip flops versus that same someone in a polo and khakis? It all depends on the situation.

Where appropriate, wear a suit; tie is optional. People generally respond better to a stranger in a suit than a stranger in a dirty shirt. In fact, the nicer you dress in public, the better people respond. Sharply dressed people seem to be less like a weirdo. Attractive people attract others.

Next, can we agree that in most cases you'll have to approach a stranger instead of them approaching you? 95% of the people you run across will be minding their own business. You can be standing in line just a few feet away from them and they won't say a thing. Pretty much everyone but Ryan.

In the beginning, I had to work up the courage to even approach someone and open my mouth. It was hard as my feet felt like they were encased in cement, and my stomach was on the floor. It was fear and self doubt. Over time, I developed a routine to get my feet out of those cement blocks. It went a little like this:

Step 1: Tell myself some of the following affirmations:

- I have power and confidence when dealing with people.
- I have value; I am worth something.
- People like me.
- I attract the best.
- I bring the best out of others.
- I am a great conversationalist.

Step 2: Hum a motivational song to myself. "Survivor" aka "Eye of the Tiger" works well.

Seriously. This is what I did. And if by the end of all that the person was still there, I'd approach. I know, it's really silly. And a few years ago, I would never have admitted this to anyone. But think about it. Did it work? Yes. Who else besides me knew? No one. So what was so embarrassing? Nothing.

Keep in mind I didn't say a hundred affirmations and sing the entire song every time. Since, you know, that would be quite long. I would say enough affirmations and hum enough of the song to get my feet moving. That was my personal "pre-game" routine. You will develop your own. If you want to borrow mine, be my guest.

Now that we have the prep-work done, there are some rules to keep in mind when you make your move:

Rule #1: Identify appropriate targets. When someone doesn't make eye contact or breaks eye contact, do not approach. If you smile at someone and they don't smile back, then they don't want to talk. Take a hint.

Keep in mind that they may not be judging you of being "not worthy" of their attention. More likely they don't even know or care that you even exist. Don't take it personally. You didn't care that they existed before either. This fact should actually give you great freedom to go about your day and try anything you want. You can take great chances, fall flat on your face, and no one will really care. People are not waiting around for you to say something truly profound or witty. It just is what it is.

If they were never looking at you in the first place, but you still want to approach, you can always try to make one or two off-hand comments to see if they engage in any conversation. If they don't respond or don't even look at you, they are not interested. Don't force it; you'll only look like a weirdo. Just move on. Remember Ryan: water off a duck's back. Try to approach someone else. No one cares that you're trying.

Rule #2: Keep the initial approach light or humorous. When you open your mouth, how does it sound if you were in the other person's shoes? I've noticed what works best are funny comments or easy non-controversial topics. Avoid world events and tragedies. Even if the building next door blew up, DO NOT talk about it at that time. You may get into it later in the conversation, but do not lead with it. You may have heard the expression: If it bleeds, it leads. That's for newscasts, not for meeting people. Stick to safe comments about mundane things. Don't be a weirdovert like in my next example. This a true story and I felt really irritated by this person.

I was in line at Starbucks one day (okay, most days) and while I was perusing the bagels and breakfast sandwiches, a lady in front of me turned around and started asking me how I felt about the situation in the Egypt. I had to get my mind from bagel to Egypt. It was quite a jarring effect. My first reaction was: Huh? What are you talking about…. So I mumbled something along the lines of "oh I'm sorry, I don't watch CNN, so I'm not really up to date on current events." And I proceeded to break eye contact. Back to the bagels. But she wouldn't let it go and went on about how sad the situation was and how she was outraged at the inhumane things going on. Awkward! I could only shrug and look at the barista for rescue.

Now remember, weirdoverts do not know they are being weird. So to keep yourself from falling into some of that behaviour, here's a helpful comparison table on the next page. I'm afraid to admit it, but I've actually said some of those things.

Everyday Topic	Suggested Comment	Weirdovert Comment
Weather/time of year	I'm glad it's still nice enough out to BBQ.	The sun isn't good for my eczema.
Upcoming holiday or significant day	I can't believe Halloween is around the corner.	What are you going to be for Halloween?
Stuff around you	Have you ever tried that muffin?	Where do pumpkins come from? Like you know what I mean?
The event you're attending	So, how'd you come to be here?	This sucks eh?

Start by asking questions or else throwing out comments that are easy for the other person to respond to. You'll want at least 2 to 3 exchanges until you can consider the ice to be broken. This lets the other person know you're not a crazy person. Remember Mark's cookies. After this, it should be safe to delve into other topics. You can possibly even introduce yourself.

Rule #3: If the other person is doing something out of the ordinary, is wearing something unusual, or is carrying something noteworthy, make a point of commenting on it.

Women generally wear cute shoes, purses, scarves, hats, earrings, and necklaces. If you're a woman, it's completely okay to start off by complimenting another woman on any of these things and ask where they got it. The wearer will totally go through the moon that someone else noticed. As a man, it's truly amazing to witness this event.

If you're a man approaching a woman, do not lead with any of these things. You will seem like you're hitting on her. Whether or not that is your intention, do not do it... you creep. Instead, stick with mundane comments first. Then after the ice has been broken (2-3 exchanges) then you can mention one (and only one) thing. The size of the ring on her finger, for example.

If you're approaching a man, it doesn't matter what your gender is. Anything works. Men always think they are being hit on. Even if he doesn't, he will love the attention. So remark away! It's okay to let him know you appreciate his choice in beer shirts. If he has an iPad and you have an iPad, go ahead and lead with that. If he's wearing sports memorabilia, ask him about the team.

The key here is to focus on the other person and not direct the conversation back to you. Take a genuine interest in what is going on in their lives and see what you can find out. Ask some questions after your initial ice breaker. Remember what we covered in the small talk chapter.

After the ice breaker, you can start to lead into a bit of those things.

Rule #4: Not every encounter will lead to a new friend. Let's face it: you can't win them all. Not everyone you talk to will want your cookie. Sometimes you only talk to a stranger for three exchanges and that's it. It's over, your lives will never intersect again.

There are a million reasons why you can't take the conversation further, and many of them have nothing to do with you, so don't take things personally.

Sometimes the other person just doesn't want to talk for whatever reason and it has nothing to do with you. You don't know what's going on in their life, so don't take offense to it.

Rule #5: Every time you try to talk to strangers, regardless of how it went, consider it a victory. You can't control how other people react. You can only control yourself and your habits so focus on that. How did you execute the process? Did you even try? Did you feel your comfort zone stretch just a little?

Every time you step out of your comfort zone, it's a victory.

A bit of warning here. Do not make the same mistake I did. For much of my life, I focused on the results instead of the process. What I found was I couldn't see results from day to day so I constantly felt like I was losing. And losing constantly is very discouraging (just ask the NHL's Edmonton Oilers). So your goal should be to only focus on things you can control. Focus on the process and eventually you can look back and you will see results.

Rule #6: You have to practice a minimum of three times a week to get better at something. Twice a week will let you maintain your level and once a week will have you constantly feeling like a beginner. This is the gist of the practice makes perfect saying. The most important aspect is being consistent on a weekly basis and being persistent by going to bat over and over again. Don't worry about the results. Remember, the highest-paid baseball players only get a hit 3 times out of 10 tries, and they are paid millions for it. Keep pushing your comfort zone. Keep trying. It all comes back to your goals. How bad do you want to change? Has that want become a need yet?

You'll want to practice as much as possible to build momentum. As you keep practicing, you will get better at talking to strangers. As you get better, you gain confidence. As you gain confidence, you'll have success. Success will motivate you to practice more. That's called momentum. Momentum will multiply your efforts meaning that it takes less effort to do the same things.

On the flip side, momentum comes and goes. You will have peaks and valleys. Take advantage of the peaks by practicing more during those times. When you're in the valleys, focus on executing the process again. Force yourself to do the uncomfortable. The goal is to reduce the time you spend in the valleys. You'll be amazed at how action will impact your mood.

That's it for the rules. However, some are more important than others. Notice, the first three rules focused on technique and the last three rules focused on the mental aspect of talking to strangers. In my opinion, I would say that the mental side is more important than the technique side. Techniques can be learned anywhere. Anyone can give you a tip to try and implement. How you are mentally while using those techniques is even more important. The image you project and confidence you exude will do more than what comes out of your mouth. Ever witness your extroverted friends talk to new people? They can say the dumbest things and yet can still connect with people.

Look at Joey on the sitcom Friends. His pickup line is "How YOU doin'?" It's so simple that it doesn't even qualify as a technique. However, the confidence he has while he says it does all the talking.

I understand that in the beginning you will need some techniques to get you started. Introverts love having "if-then" rules. It uses fewer brain cells and thus lowers the risk of your brain short-circuiting and blanking out. By having techniques to use you will have some success, which leads to confidence. I get it, but I bring it up so that you are aware that technique does not make an ambivert.

Technique doesn't change your core inner being. Your state of mind does. Remember, you're reconstructing your personality to what you want it to be. By being in the correct frame of mind for long periods, you will start to internalize it and become it. You are what you think you are. As Buddha once taught:

"The mind is everything. What you think you become."

In summary:

1. Dress sharp.
2. Do your pre-game routine.
3. Identify appropriate targets to approach.
4. Keep it light or humorous.
5. Make note and comment on something unusual or unique about the other person.
6. Not every encounter will lead to a new friend.
7. The very act of trying is a victory.
8. Practice at least 3-times a week, every week.
9. Keep your goals in mind.

Edwin's Thoughts

Other than Vy Tri's inappropriate comment about the Edmonton Oilers, he is so right. His cookie analogy is great and memorable. You can even flip his example around and make the goal of the conversation to get them to offer you one of their cookies!

When Vy Tri talked about telling yourself some affirmations, I immediately thought of the Saturday Night Live sketch of Stuart Smalley. He would sit in front of the mirror and tell himself that he was "good enough, smart enough and doggone it, people like me." While cheesy, it is true. We are all worth it. We are all likeable, and we all want to be liked. So spend time finding ways to like yourself and to also like others.

I like to talk to other people because they know things I don't. I'm insanely curious about life and the best way to learn is from others. As a young man, I thought I knew everything but as I've gotten older I've realized that there is more that I don't know. Others have different life experiences and so think differently. Finding what makes them tick fascinates me and is part of why I like people.

However, like most introverts, I don't want to talk all the time. I need my space so when a weirdovert comes up and throws themselves into my space and won't leave, I get irritated. That will be you at some point. You will try to start a conversation and it will flop. The other person just isn't into interactions at that time. So what? It doesn't have anything to do with you. Something that helps me when I get rebuffed from starting a conversation is thinking that their spouse or significant other probably yelled at them this morning. Regardless of its truth, it really helps me move on from the event.

My easiest conversation starter is when I comment on something interesting about the other person. If someone is reading a book it's because they are interested in the topic or someone recommended it. I've found that many people want to share their ideas, if for no other reason than it makes them confirm to themselves that the time they are investing in the book is worth it. If someone is wearing something with a sports team's logo on it, they are usually passionate or at least have a story about why they got that shirt or ball cap.

Selling for Ambiverts
By Edwin

Becoming an ambivert is about having more control over your life and the impact you make. Whether at work, your church, at your kid's school, or just among your friends, ambiverts are less on the periphery and more involved and influential.

As Vy Tri talked about, creating connections start with convincing someone to take a cookie. In reality, you are selling that cookie, and then selling them yourself, your ideas, your product, or your friendship.

As a parent, you sell your kids on eating their vegetables, doing their homework, being quiet, and going to bed. As a teacher, you sell your students on sitting still, listening, learning, and studying. As a coach, you sell your players on training hard, doing the drill right, eating right, and buying into the system. As a doctor, you sell your patients on the importance of taking their medicine, exercising, and eating well. As an employee, you sell your boss on listening to your ideas, adopting a new strategy, keeping your job, or getting a raise. As a spouse, you sell your spouse on the idea of having sex, not having sex, parenting, spending money, saving money, or getting a dog. The list can go on.

Every day you sell.

Introverts struggle because they don't engage others. They don't initiate conversations. They don't feel confident enough to express their opinions. They don't connect with others in a way that demonstrates that they actually care.

Extroverts struggle because they don't come across as sincere. They talk too much. They don't pay enough attention to the other person.

According to Daniel Pink in his book, *To Sell is Human*, success is an inverted U shaped curve with the introversion/extroversion spectrum along the bottom and sales success along the vertical axis. Studies show that introverts and extroverts are equally good at sales. However, the most successful sales people are in the middle, those elusive ambiverts that we keep talking about.

Being in the middle works.

While we aren't talking about sales per se, we are talking about having more control and impact in your life. We are talking about moving others and making a difference.

Based on the preceding chapters, you've learned to initiate conversations and have that requisite small talk that creates connections with others. Now that you can talk to people, let's talk about the next step in persuading, influencing, and convincing others.

In his book *The Talent Code,* Daniel Coyle explains that the best way to learn is to focus on what you are doing wrong and make it better. He uses the example of figure skaters that either practice to perfect the jump they can already do or fix the one they struggle with. The skaters that win are those that practice what they can't do.

So to start, think about the types of persuading, convincing, and influencing that you do every day. Who are you trying to influence on a regular basis? It could be your spouse, children, co-workers, bosses, employees, customers, or prospective clients.

Vy Tri and I did a lot of fumbling combined with trial and error in our own journeys. But we are going to borrow the ABC's from Dan Pink's book *To Sell Is Human* for three areas of focus to enhance your introverted gifts and build your extroverted muscle.

- Attunement: It's all about them.
- Buoyancy: Get used to rejection.
- Clarity: Explain so they understand.

First a couple of clarifying points. The ABCs are not meant to be taken in this order. They are three distinct skill sets that you need to work on individually. And you will never be perfect at these. It's a learning curve, and one that never ends.

Attunement

In any conversation, there are two perspectives:

1. What's going on in your own head.
2. What's going on in their head.

The first perspective is easy. It's human nature to be in our own head – we know what we are thinking, feeling, and where we want to go with the conversation. For introverts, that occupies much of our brain space when in an actual conversation.

But it's hard to get into the other person's head and see the second perspective. It's actually why both extroverts and introverts are bad at selling. Both personality types are so into their own story or conversation that they don't take the time to really listen to the other person.

Make it all about them.

Over the years, I've become better at small talk and finding points of commonality with someone. I'm insanely curious and love information. In my 20's, like most young men, I thought I knew it all. I was the smartest guy in the room. Over time, I've realized that nothing is further from the truth. Everyone has a unique perspective because they grew up differently. Their political, sociological, religious, and economic views make sense given where they came from. So rather than think that I know better, I want to learn what makes others tick.

I remember meeting a couple who were looking for a new advisor. We spent a few minutes talking about books we had recently read. From there we moved onto their financial situation.

I spent a number of minutes educating them, but about 10 minutes in, I lost them. Their eyes glazed over a bit and they stopped asking as many questions. I got too in-depth with the detail and we lost our connection. Their feelings of comfort went away and by the end of the meeting, there wasn't enough connection for them to like me. I did the small talk but not the sales.

As I reflected on that conversation, it had become less about them and more about what I did. They didn't care about what I did. They cared about what I could do for them. There is a difference. A former boss of mine explained it as the GQs and the OBs. I spent my time on the GQs or General Qualities of what I did instead of the OBs or Owner Benefits. I didn't focus on the client. What are they looking for? What do they need? What would highly benefit them?

Here, introverts have an advantage. They have tremendous capacity to see into another person's head because they spend so much time in their own head. "Know thyself" is an ancient Delphic maxim inscribed on the walls of the

Temple of Apollo. It has a variety of meanings, but to me, it's that in knowing the real me, I have a better capacity to understand others.

If you don't know where you are coming from and how complicated the motivations can be for the things you do or buy, then how can you understand where the other person is coming from? The first step in attunement is therefore to spend time thinking about yourself. Weird comment? Let me explain further.

A therapist introduced me to the concept of self-awareness and self-compassion. He explained that one of the key parts to having compassion for others is to first have self-compassion. If we are critical of ourselves, then it's easier to be critical of others. If we have self-compassion, it's easier to have compassion for others.

Many studies have shown that the way we view others and ourselves is markedly different. When we do something bad like cut someone off in traffic, it's because we are late for an important meeting. When someone cuts us off, it's because they are an asshole. When our temper blows up at someone, it's because all these little things added up to a point where we couldn't take it anymore. When someone blows up at us, it's because they are an asshole. When we disagree with someone's opinion, it's because we have lots of knowledge on a subject and have carefully thought out our idea. When someone disagrees with us, it's because they are an asshole.

Get the picture?

And the flip side is also true. When we do something kind, it's because we are a really nice person. When someone else does something nice to us, we think it's because they are having a good day.

This is called the attribution bias. We think our good actions are because we are good at heart and our bad actions are because of our circumstances. And when we judge others, we feel their good actions are because of good circumstances and their bad actions are because of character flaws.

So this first step of attunement is recognizing that our own motivations are complex and therefore other's motivations are also complex. The reasons for their actions are rarely simple and it always makes sense for them. So attunement is about honestly and genuinely putting yourself in their shoes, not thinking "well if I were them I would…"

I can't begin to stress this point enough. It's not that we have to figure out how to get them to think like us. It's actually about understanding them. Believing them. Knowing them. Getting them.

Spending this time and effort may help you know them better than they know themselves. They may not realize why they are reacting the way they do – but you can sense it. And you don't need to tell them about it, just recognize that it's just a part of who they are.

When you do the small talk right, you get to know them. One of my favourite books of all time is Dale Carnegie's *How to Win Friends and Influence People* because he talks about the key principle being to "really like people." If you don't like others, they can tell. So cultivate an interest in others, not because it's part of your job, but because people are fascinating and they are worth it.

Attunement is about liking other people.

This can be a real struggle for introverts. It was for me. I spend so much time in my own head that I kind of enjoy it there. It's easy to get lost in my own world and believe that the only truth in life is mine.

And that is natural. Watch kids – the majority of them are so in their own head it's crazy. My oldest, Carson, is often clueless about the rest of the world, just like each of us were when we were his age. The only reality is his. It's the difference between being a kid and being mature. Some of us grow out of it and some never do.

What little I know about teenagers, is they are the ultimate example of people who live only in their own heads. It's a real sign of growth and maturity when you can move beyond yourself and become part of the world, not just live in your own.

My challenge to you is no different. Move on from living in your own head and get into others. Be interested in them. It's hard work and it's fascinating at the same time. What would it be like to be a woman? What would it be like to grow up as the youngest child? What would it be like to grow up with divorced parents? What would it be like to_____?

Get curious. A famous English story goes like this.

> A woman in England went on separate dates with two very famous people who had very different personalities, William Gladstone and Benjamin Disraeli.
>
> Asked about her evening with Gladstone she said,
>
> "He took me to the symphony and by the end of the night I felt like I was with the most sophisticated and smartest man in the world."
>
> And how about your evening with Disraeli her friends asked.
>
> "He took me to the opera. By the end of the night I felt like I was the most sophisticated and smartest woman in the world."
>
> Gladstone spent the evening talking about himself.
>
> Disraeli spent his evening listening to her. Disraeli made her feel great.

People like you more when they get to talk about themselves. They don't necessarily want to hear your story but love to tell their own. If at the end of the conversation, they feel listened to, then they are more likely to like you.

It's a peculiarity of human nature but one that you can use to your advantage.

Believing that your client's perspective is more important than yours separates the sleazy car salesman from the trusted advisor. It's the final part of attunement.

The sleazy used car salesman is trying to sell you a vehicle because it results in income for him. He cares more about the sale than about what is best for you. When you leave an interaction with him, you feel that he got the best of the transaction. You have a lingering sense of unease about the whole thing.

However, if you enter every interaction genuinely wanting what is best for the other person, then your relationships and interactions will be very different. Your true motivation will come across.

Solve their problem, not yours. Help them. Make it all about them.

Then it will not seem like sales at all – and it isn't. You are becoming a problem solver. You will be making a difference in the world. You will become a better person because the people you interact with will actually like you and want to have a continued relationship with you. This means not just one sale, but a relationship that has the potential to blossom into something more.

For people who are not selling a product but influencing others, like teachers, doctors, or parents, the same principles apply. Malcolm Gladwell, in his book *David and*

Goliath, writes about teachers who are good at classroom management.

Successful teachers are not those that can get a class under control once it's gone haywire, but rather those who sense the beginning of an undercurrent of unease and stop it from snowballing into something chaotic. Great teachers are hyper aware of what is going on in the classroom. They are always thinking about what their children are doing and finding ways to keep them engaged. They are looking at the class from the student's point of view and seeing what the children are seeing.

The less successful teacher tries to control their class through authoritarian means. They use adult techniques like threats and punishments to run the classroom, with rules that adults would respond to. But they are not teaching adults. They are teaching kids. 8-year olds are not defiant by nature, but they are easily bored. Children want to be engaged with what's going on.

The same is true of successful parents. They can pause from their own daily challenges and see what life is like for a 16 year old. Teenagers don't have the years of experience to sort through what's really important in life and so they make a big deal about the strangest things. Successful parents can meet their children in their world and engage them there.

To sum up attunement, it's about liking other people. It's about understanding them and their motivations. And it's about wanting what's best for others regardless of what's in it for you.

Buoyancy

B is about buoyancy. Buoyancy starts and ends with your beliefs about your own self worth. This is usually something that extroverts are better at than us.

One of my favourite quotes is:

Fall down seven times, get up eight.

We could debate how one can get up eight times when falling down only seven, but the principle is that you keep getting up. It's learning to acknowledge that some interactions will not be good. When you put yourself out there by making a suggestion, selling a product, or trying to influence a behaviour, some people will not buy it. They will not accept what you are trying to say.

We usually don't put ourselves out there because it's risky. However, we are also not giving ourselves the opportunity to succeed.

There are three parts to buoyancy.

First, get ready for rejection. I watched an interesting video on *30 Days of Rejection Therapy* by Mark Moschel. Each day for a month, he had to ask someone a question that he knew would result in rejection. The questions had to be slightly outrageous, to ensure that he got 'no' for an answer.

As the month went on, it got easier to ask these questions as he built up a stronger and stronger buoyancy muscle. He even started enjoying the asking and getting rejected.

And like any muscle, as soon as he quit asking, the muscle atrophied. Within a few weeks of not asking outrageous questions, he felt uncomfortable approaching strangers. I experience the same thing at work. When I'm in the groove, calling potential clients gets easier and easier as I do it every day. But if I stop making these calls for a period of time (usually over the summer when I spend more time with my family), it's hard to get started up again. Buoyancy is a muscle you can build up, but you have to keep working on it to keep it strong.

Buoyancy is a muscle that gets stronger over time.

Second, realize that when others reject you, it's rarely personal. Other people don't say "no" just because they want to hurt you. They are only thinking about themselves. It has absolutely nothing to do with you. If you are attuned to them, you will believe that if you were in their shoes, you would also say no. They are only making decisions that are logical to them.

Third, you have to believe in yourself. Believe that you are doing a good thing. Believe in your product, service, or idea. If it's going to be good for most people, then keep on keeping on. If you don't believe in what you are selling, then that will slowly erode at your self-esteem and feelings of integrity.

You have to believe in yourself. You have to want the best for the person who answers that door. If you sell vacuums, you have to believe that you have the world's best vacuum, and most people could use a cleaner house because it's healthier. If you are a parent, you want what's best for your teenager, and you really want to help them.

Buoyancy is hard because it's a rare person who enjoys rejection. It's a hard skill to learn. Even the most hardened salesperson will struggle with this feeling on a particularly bad day. As an introvert, it's especially important to get out of your own head. We are more inclined to let our little gremlins tell us all the reasons that the rejection was personal and that we aren't worthy of the job we are doing.

There are many things you can do to get out from under these feelings. Drinking isn't one of them. Wallowing isn't either. The successful people I know use one or more of these techniques:

1. Spend some time doing something you are already good at (a sport, blogging, visiting with close friends, reading). This will help restore some confidence in yourself.

2. Meditate. Part of meditation is the ability to learn mindfulness, learning to be present in the moment. Being mindful helps you learn to recognize your own unease and work with it, instead of letting rejection feel personal. It

also helps you separate out the useful inner voices from those that hinder your work.

3. Talk to a friend or colleague. When you talk to others, putting your feelings into words seems to be cathartic. It also helps get you out of crazy talk. When you verbalize your thoughts to someone else, the crazy ideas will start to seem less true.

Like exercising a muscle, buoyancy is a mental state that gets stronger over time. The more you face rejection and move past it, the easier it gets.

Clarity

Introverts usually know exactly what they are trying to say and it makes so much sense. *Why can't the other person get it!*

It's not about the words you use. It's about the words they hear.

Clarity builds on attunement. Clarity is all about what the other person is hearing and understanding, not about what you are saying. Clarity is about getting inside the other person's head (attunement) and listening to the words that are coming out of your mouth.

Clarity is not about repeating things to make your point. It's not about finding better words to explain what you are trying to say. It is not about speaking louder than the other person.

Clarity is knowing what you are trying to sell. It is being crystal clear about your own product, service, or idea. Why do you believe in what you have? Why do you think it's good? Why do you think it's good for them? And these beliefs have to be internalized because you can't fake it.

We've all heard the adage that communication is 90% non-verbal. Your body language will betray you if you aren't 100% committed to your product, service, or goal. This means that your body language is important if not critical.

We've evolved with the subconscious ability to read non-verbal cues. It's all part of our fight, flight, or freeze hardwiring. In order to survive, our ancestors learned to evaluate every encounter with a stranger as quickly as possible. Our brain still does that, even though in North America, our society has advanced past the need to worry about tigers jumping out of bushes or enemies hiding in trees.

When you are explaining the benefits of a widget to a client, they are subconsciously reading your body language. They are evaluating your belief in what you are selling. Are you fascinated or engaged? Are you bored? Are you telling the truth? They may not be able to consciously tell you why they think you are telling the truth or telling a lie, but they get a feeling.

Being boring and stiff is ineffective. If the speaker isn't personally moved by their message, then why should we be moved? If they can't get emotionally involved in the ideas they are spreading, then why should it matter to us?

It has to be real. We can all think of times when we've been listening to someone who is passionate. Whether it's the local sports team, driverless cars, flu vaccines, government waste, or scrap booking, a topic is way more interesting when the speaker cares about it. They get lost in their own head and go into a mini rant on the subject.

So believe in your product or service. Internalize why you are sticking your neck out to attach your name to it. Know that this is the best thing for them.

The next step is learning to communicate well. We've talked about how to start and have social conversations. Now you need to learn to hear what they are hearing. It's not about the words you use. It's about the words they hear. Can you boil down what you have to say into something that can be understood?

People learn in many different ways. Some learn best by way of story, others by facts, and still others by visuals. I've learned to incorporate all three into every explanation. That way, when I have a couple in a meeting, I am more likely to get both of their attentions.

It's also about using well-chosen words and not jargon. It's about painting pictures with words that help them remember the point that you were trying to make. It's about drawing things on paper that you can leave with them so they can refer back to it and trigger memories.

Clarity is about both the head and the heart. Logic alone will never win people over – you have to create an attachment to their emotions too.

You have to make sure that your pitch makes sense. If it's incomprehensible, then you will get nowhere. The listener will be spending more time trying to work out the details of your pitch rather than thinking about whether your idea or product will work for them.

Think about your story from the perspective of someone who doesn't know as much as you. What are their life experiences and what are they hearing? This comes back to attunement (it seems to always come back to attunement).

In this case, you have to get out of your own head and into theirs. Clarity is about being able to articulate their story first. Being able to reframe what the other person is saying. Can you clearly show that you know what they want, what they are looking for, and what they are feeling?

When arguing with someone, it can sometimes devolve into each of us repeating our own opinions louder and louder until we agree to disagree. Despite knowing better, it's so much easier to fall back into the arguing habits we learned as kids on the playground. Unfortunately, this usually solves nothing. Instead, the proper technique is to listen to their side, repeat it back to them, and explain why they think the way they do to see if you really get it. Show that you understand their side of the story.

You will know that you do this well when someone turns to you and says that you are describing their position better than they could have themselves!

Then talk about points where you both agree. Show that you understand the issues. Being able to step back and see the big picture is a real skill. Especially if you can articulate the big picture that isn't biased but an objective look at the discussion. Pretend there is a third party sitting there that is listening in and trying to understand.

Only when you can show that you know their side of the story can you start explaining your side. And accept the fact that the other person may not put in the same effort as you just did. But because you made the effort, you've increased the chances that they will make the same effort. They feel understood and will want to reciprocate by listening to you too.

When it comes to kids, it's much harder. Adults have the benefit of years of experience. We know what is really important in most cases. When in kindergarten, my son regularly freaked out because he couldn't make the letter 'A' properly. It wouldn't erase entirely and crossing it out and just redoing it wasn't an option. In his world, this was so important and had to be perfect.

If I dismiss his feelings, there is no conversation. Listening and calming him down is the only thing to do. Then we can start talking.

In summary

- Attunement: It's all about them.
- Buoyancy: Get used to rejection.
- Clarity: Explain so they understand.

Vy Tri's Thoughts

As Edwin said above, keep things simple. There are thousands of books on sales techniques, and most of them are great. However, after you've read a few, you'll find a common thread. The concept of the ABCs is the basics. Follow them and you'll have success when you need to persuade someone to your point of view.

I always emphasize the need to connect with the other person through some form of shared experience, acquaintance, belief, or preference. Make eye contact and turn their words into questions. Dig deep. The more they talk and the more you uncover, the more potential ways you have to nudge them to your point of view. If they think they got there by themselves, you've just solved a lot of your problems. It's always best to get your customer to sell themselves.

There are generally two types of sales people: facilitators and motivators. Facilitators layout all the facts and help you make an educated decision. They help you weigh the pros and cons and ultimately decide what is best in your circumstances. Most people respond well to this type of sales because it's logic-based and low-pressure.

However, the second type of sales person is just as effective. Motivators use emotional attachment, nice sounding words, and pretty pictures to persuade you to buy. Many TV commercials use the motivator form of selling. It works because we are emotional beings.

It's not a question of one form being better than the other, as each of us, by nature, responds better to one method. If you're trying to influence someone, you have to identify which selling language the person prefers. If you try to motivate a facilitator, you'll come across as a pushy sales person. If you try to facilitate a motivator, you'll come across as a boring egghead.

Personally, I thought I was a facilitator. After all, it's what any intelligent person should want, right? But in fact, I have discovered that I prefer being motivated. As you can tell, emotional connection is what I'm all about. Edwin is definitely a facilitator.

Another thing is to keep in mind that all behaviour makes sense when you think about it from the other person's point of view. All seemingly crazy or nonsensical behaviour has its roots in logic. You just have to identify it. For example, I saw a TV show that highlighted a huge marital conflict because the wife insisted that all paper bags in the house needed to be shoved in the space between the refrigerator and the cabinets. It was an eyesore in a relatively nice looking kitchen. After digging into her story, the counselor discovered that her mother always did that because her grandmother always did that. Why? Because a long time ago, the paper bags were thought to make refrigerators more efficient and save money for the family. We can see that the behaviour makes sense if we know the back-story. All behaviour has its roots in logic.

I could probably conclude there, but I'm going to do the "One More Thing" again. Colin Johnston is a former boss of mine and one of my mentors. He taught me the most important lesson in sales. And that's what I want to leave you with in this chapter as it ties in Attunement, Buoyancy, and Clarity. To be effective at sales, you must distinguish between objections and stalls. An objection can be handled, but a stall cannot. An objection is a logical challenge to what you are offering. These can be overcome with facts. For example, the objection can be: "Your price is too high." You can get past that with more facts and information. Whereas a very common stall is: "I don't have time right now." You cannot overcome this with any amount of information. It's not a real objection. Many sales people take this stall at face value and try to address it with persuasion and clarity. All you're doing there is annoying your prospect. What you need to do is focus on attunement and get to the core objection. Colin taught me the most effective way to do this is to simply ask: "Is there something about this that just doesn't sit right with you?" That is a question you can use directly with a client. There's no wrong answer because you're asking about their feelings. In a business to business setting, you might instead ask: "Do you see any value in this?" Follow that up with "That's fair. Tell me more about that." Now listen to the answer (that's buoyancy). If you did it right, your prospect will tell you the real objection. Now you have a tangible concern you can address (with clarity).

Putting It All Together

So far, we've been telling you what we did on our own ambivert journeys and some ideas to maybe help you on your own journey. So we thought it would be interesting to conclude the book with how we both function as ambiverts today.

Just to get the semantics out of the way, we are not "done" our own journeys, but we are well within the ambivert part of the continuum. Our respective journeys now involve refinement more than making big changes in personality traits. To use an analogy, it's like working out at the gym. We've already gained the muscle mass we want, but we keep going to the gym in order to tone and sculpt that muscle. We are constantly learning and growing as ambiverts.

Ambiversion

For Vy Tri, he started out eschewing his introverted side to become a full-on extrovert. This lead to prolonged stay in the weirdovert stage. It wasn't until he embraced his introvert side that he was able to settle into true ambiversion.

Edwin took the approach of trying to add extroverted behaviours at the appropriate times while maintaining his introversion. Being extroverted is still a lot of work but he has learned to embrace and enjoy those moments more.

Small Talk

Vy Tri has gotten to a point where he doesn't have to use the "interesting" trick as much. Instead he asks engaging follow-up questions. The focus stays on the other person and the goal is still to seek out more information. Vy Tri isn't actively looking for spots to jump-in on the conversation and hijack it. However, he isn't opposed to it either. If Vy Tri has a great story to go with the most recent subject matter, but the other person hasn't stopped talking, Vy Tri doesn't interrupt. He let's the other person continue talking. At a later time, when there is a pause, he takes that opportunity to tell his story. "Going back to what you were saying earlier…"

Through years of practice, Vy Tri doesn't have to prepare and rehearse new stories much anymore. All that practice has given him the ability to "wing-it." Sure, sometimes the delivery and timing needs work, but he makes mental notes and corrects them on the fly the next time the story is told. By retelling stories over and over, he can actually watch the reaction of the audience, adjust the rhythm, and make appropriate embellishments during the recounting.

Small talk is still a challenge for Edwin. He's very impatient and likes to get to the meat of an issue or talk about serious topics. He would rather settle down with a drink and go into deep conversations right away. This makes him come across as very intense and makes him jump into weightier issues too soon. This reveals his introvert side.

Because small talk isn't something he loves, finding commonalities or threads to keep small talk conversations flowing is a lot of work. He can manage, but it is incredibly draining. It's why at parties and large group events, if he can't get immersed in a serious discussion, he needs to set aside time to be alone and regenerate some of his spent energy.

Talking to Strangers

Edwin loves to talk to strangers. There are so many interesting things to learn from them. His curiosity about life and people makes him hyperaware to what's going on around him so he finds lots of ways to open up conversations. Where are they from? What are they doing here? Who are they connected to? He's quick to ask lots of questions and be interested in the other person. This genuine interest is a huge asset.

In the past, Edwin would try to jump into a group by being an extrovert, but all that happened was his weirdovert would show up instead. So these days, Edwin tries to blend in with the group until the opportunity arises to interact in some smaller way with one or two individuals. He's found that in most cases, it is just better to be an active listener and be appreciated for that. It's an easier skill to learn and works just as well. After all, not everyone needs to be the life of the party.

The biggest change Vy Tri has found is that he doesn't have to do the pre-game routine anymore. He's comfortable talking to strangers, especially in small groups. This evolution can be attributed to his focus on other people. He's become blind to his own insecurities in these situations. Vy Tri finds these interactions mentally stimulating and seeks to add value to others. Baring that, he just wants to give them a good laugh.

Vy Tri still has trouble in larger groups and in groups where he's the new guy. He's found that the best thing to do in these cases is to talk to the first person who makes eye contact, and admit that he's new and doesn't know anyone. This typically leads to multiple introductions. If he brings a friend, he's careful not to use the friend as a crutch. He will resist cocooning in a corner with the friend.

Sales

Attunement, Buoyancy, and Clarity have become a core part of Vy Tri's mental make-up. He views sales as a series of relationships based on trust and credibility. The relationship is the foundation on which sales is based. This is attunement. Clarity results from doing the attunement step correctly and also by focusing in on what the other person really wants. Boil it down to clear needs. Vy Tri has a lot of buoyancy in that he lets things roll of his back and rolls with the punches. Obviously, self-confidence has a lot to do with this, but what really helps is having the ability to separate himself from the actual sales. The other person isn't rejecting him personally, he or she is only rejecting the solution being presented. Picture three parties to any potential sales transaction: the buyer on one side of the table, the seller on the other and the solution in the middle of the table. Vy Tri as the seller, tries as much as possible to move his chair to the same side of the table as the buyer. He wants to create a situation where both he and the seller are looking at the solution together. If it works out, great. If it doesn't work out, also great. They both tried to find the solution together and it just didn't happen. There's no bad-guy here and no hurt feelings. But he's created a friend during the process.

Edwin's biggest change over the last few years is in attunement. As a young man, he felt that other's opinions were incomplete, ill-informed, or just plain wrong. Today, he recognizes that everyone has a valid opinion given their unique backgrounds. People believe different things because of their different life experiences. Therefore, they have a point and it's worth exploring and understanding. Maybe through clarity and conversation, that opinion can change – but it doesn't have to. Instead, Edwin joins with the other party to find out what they really need and then helping them find it.

Clarity is another growth area for Edwin. He's very linear in his thinking so the way he explains things does not work for everyone. He's realized it is not about using better words or repeating them over and over. It's not "the facts, just the facts, and only the facts." Clarity is about everything. It's about meeting the other person where they are and talking in a way that they understand. Both from an emotional and from a logical point of view. Learning the names for these three skills has really helped Edwin in his sales interactions. He now recognizes these as steps in the process of helping people.

Wrap Up

We have many differences in how we became ambiverts. And today, as you've read in these pages, we are different flavours of ambivert. But we have many commonalities that we think should ring true for anyone who becomes an ambivert:

- We genuinely care about and like other people.
- We went through the awkwardvert and weirdovert stages.
- We now have large and varied networks as a by-product of our journey.
- We love both sides of our personality.
- We need down time to recharge.

Your journey to ambiversion will be your own because ambiversion encompasses a whole range of people. Your results will be your own. Your motivations will be your own. But the process will be similar. We sincerely hope this book gives you some ways to shortcut your journey.

Our entire goal in this book is to make the process shorter and less painful (though it won't be painless). As we've said many times, use this book as if it's a grocery store: buy what you need now and leave the rest. Then come back again as you develop different needs.

Have fun shopping!

Join Us

This may be the end of the book, but not the end of the conversation. Please join us on Facebook (facebook.com/ambivertjourney) and share your story.

As you can tell, we love stories. We think everyone has a truly marvellous tale to tell. Your story has to be better than ours. Neither one of us had a murder mystery or a car chase in our stories. Even if you had a pretty pedestrian journey (doubtful) we still want to hear from you. What you went through may be just the magic that allows another reader to break through their own barriers. For example, your unique viewpoint on a "pre-game routine" might be all it takes to unlock someone's ability to talk to strangers.

Most of all, we want your weirdovert stories. Or rather your weirdovert confessions! Don't forget the weirdovert conversions! You can even write in about weirdoverts you know and love. (Please change the names and any identifying traits.) We can all learn a lot from weirdoverts. They're like a twisted mirror of our own personalities.

And finally, we would totally value your honest feedback about this book. What did we do well? How can we improve the next version?

Please reach out and be part of this new community.

Printed in Great Britain
by Amazon